THE GREAT LIVES SERIES

Great Lives biographies shed an exciting new light on the many dynamic men and women whose actions, visions, and dedication to an ideal have influenced the course of history. Their ambitions, dreams, successes and failures, the controversies they faced and the obstacles they overcame are the true stories behind these distinguished world leaders, explorers, and great Americans.

Other biographies in the Great Lives Series

MIKHAIL GORBACHEV: The Soviet Innovator

JOHN F. KENNEDY: Courage in Crisis

ABRAHAM LINCOLN: The Freedom President

SALLY RIDE: Shooting for the Stars

HARRIET TUBMAN: Call to Freedom

ACKNOWLEDGMENT

A special thanks to educators Dr. Frank Moretti, Ph.D., Associate Headmaster of the Dalton School in New York City; Dr. Paul Mattingly, Ph.D., Professor of History at New York University; and Barbara Smith, M. S., Assistant Superintendent of the Los Angeles Unified School District, for their contributions to the Great Lives Series.

GREAT LIVES

CHRISTOPHER COLUMBUS
THE INTREPID MARINER

Sean J. Dolan

FAWCETT COLUMBINE
NEW YORK

For middle school readers

A Fawcett Columbine Book
Published by Ballantine Books

Library of Congress Catalogue Card Number: 89-90817

ISBN: 0-449-90393-1

Cover design and illustration by Paul Davis

Manufactured in the United States of America

First Edition: September 1989

10 9 8 7 6 5 4 3 2 1

TABLE OF CONTENTS

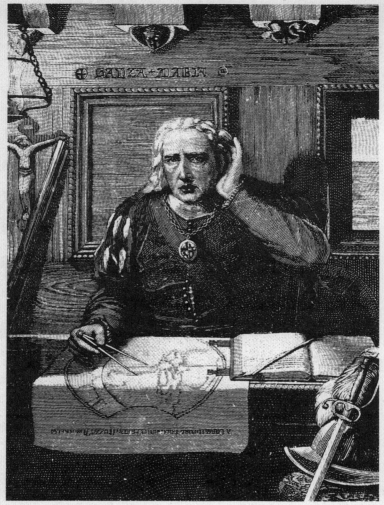

Christopher Columbus in his cabin aboard the caravel Santa Maria, hearing his men shouting, "Land! Land!" Columbus thought he had discovered the long-sought western route to Asia, but in fact he had reached lands then unknown to Europeans— the Americas.

1

The Captain General
Takes Charge

ONCE AGAIN THE night was mild, the sea was calm, and the giant sailing vessel, the *Santa María*, raced along. Her captain, Christopher Columbus, was well-pleased with her progress. Since leaving the Canary Islands, an archipelago located off the northwest coast of Africa, the *Santa María* and her sister ships, the *Niña* and the *Pinta*, had made remarkable time. Over the past five days, as Columbus had just finished noting in his ship's log, the *Santa María* had maintained an average speed of eight knots. Other ship captains considered five knots in such latitudes to be adequate speed.

Columbus shut the log and placed it in the heavy chest that sailors used to store their belongings while at sea. He looked at his quarters. A similar log, an apparent duplicate of the one he had just finished writing in, lay on top of the crude wooden table that served as his desk. It shared the tabletop with a leather-bound Bible. A crimson ribbon held the Bible open to a page in the Old Testament's Book of Isaiah, where Columbus had underscored a particular passage: "The isle saw it, and feared; the ends of the earth were afraid, drew near, and came." In an age characterized by intense religious devotion, the depths of Columbus's faith made him special. The Biblical passage, like others that he had singled out, provided the captain with solace on his long journey and served as the justification for the extraordinary adventure he was embarked upon.

Next to the Bible was a well-thumbed copy of *Imago Mundi,* a geographical and theological treatise by the French writer Pierre d'Ailly. Columbus read *Imago Mundi* most nights, and his confidence was bolstered by the learned Frenchman's claim that Asia could be reached in a few days by sailing west from Africa. The weighty volume rested atop nautical charts, on which Columbus charted his own progress and consulted the reckonings of other mariners.

Columbus snuffed out the candle that lit his small cabin and stepped forth onto the deck. High above the *Santa María*'s three masts a thin line of clouds drifted across the face of the full moon. The drifting clouds gave the illusion that the moon, too, was speeding toward the west. Columbus considered it a good omen, one more sign that the heavens themselves favored this journey. Thousands of stars twinkled in the sky. There were more stars by far than could be seen from even the highest roof-top in Genoa, Italy, or Lisbon, Spain, the cities where Columbus had spent most of his days when not at sea. There were more stars, too, than he'd seen on any of his earlier voyages. They stretched all the way to the horizons at all four points of the compass. It was as if, Columbus thought, in jour-neying to uncharted regions of the earth, he'd been allowed a glimpse of heaven. The star-filled skies might have filled another man with a sense of his own insignificance and of the precariousness of his situation. The *Santa María* and her sister vessels were now nearly one month's sailing time beyond the nearest known land. No one knew how many days of sailing there would be before the ships reached land. The three small ships, manned by only ninety sailors, lay adrift on the vast and power-ful ocean. But Columbus was reassured by the numberless stars above him, and by the broad and restless expanse of sea that surrounded him. It was not mere bravery that gave him the assurance to continue, but faith. Columbus believed that the awe-inspiring beauty that surrounded him could only be the handiwork of the one true God, and he felt secure in his Lord and Savior's protection. If only my crewmen shared my belief, Columbus thought. They were devout, of course, and like most Spanish they were good Catholics, faithful in their recitation of their morning prayers. However, they were also superstitious, poorly educated, and fearful.

On board ship, on this night, Columbus's senses exulted. He delighted in the sting and tang of the salt spray. The creaking of the riggings rang like chimes to his ears. The full-breasted swell of the sails thrilled him more than any great work of art. Even the hardships of shipboard life — the uncomfortable quarters, the unsanitary conditions, the salty water, the monotonous diet of salt-preserved meat, dried peas, and the hard wheat biscuit known as hardtack — did not bother him. Again, it was his faith that gave him the strength to endure such discomforts. As his body grew lean and his skin coarsened from the limited diet, and as his white hair grew long and unruly, he thought of the many saints and martyrs who had suffered for their religious beliefs. Next to their suffering, his own trials seemed unimportant.

However, Columbus's men did not share his outlook toward suffering. The mission had scared most of them. From the beginning, few believed that one could sail west, across the perilous Ocean Sea, to the East. They did not believe that they could reach the fabled Indies, where, it was said, the Great Khan's robes were trimmed with precious stones and the palaces were roofed with gold. A few brave sailors had signed on for the glory of the journey, but most had shipped out with Columbus because their desire for wealth had gotten the better of their cowardice. Columbus even had to get the queen's permission to release criminals from jail and promise them pardons in order to round out the crew!

For the first ten days of the voyage, the ships made brilliant time. The sun shone brightly. The winds were favorable. "What a delight was the savor of the mornings," Columbus wrote in his log. Soon after, though, the crew became uneasy. They had believed that ten days' sailing would bring them to Antilia, an island believed to be located in the middle of the Ocean Sea. When they failed to reach the island, the little faith they had in their captain's mission disappeared.

Columbus noticed that the members of the crew had grown sullen and were slow in obeying his orders. They whispered among themselves, breaking off in silence at his approach. Columbus knew what was going through their minds: that Cathay (China), Cipangu (Japan), and the other mysterious lands of the Indies were not 2,400 miles away, as he had told them, but 10,000 miles away! The most ignorant of them doubted the existence of Asia and believed the earth to be flat. They thought that their ships would fall off the earth if they sailed too close to the edge. Why, Columbus mused, these men knew no more of geography than the mapmakers of the Dark Ages, who decorated the unknown regions of the world with fanciful drawings of hideous creatures and the inscription "Here there be monsters."

The date that night was October 5, 1492. There had been no sign of land, and fresh water was in short supply. The men were surly and restless. Columbus had been on enough voyages to know the danger of mutiny. It was like a virus or plague that could infect an entire ship in no time. Only the best and the bravest sailors were immune to it. Under its spell even the smallest inconvenience was unbearable, and the defiance of a single sailor could plunge the entire ship into rebellion. Still, there had been no outright disobedience, at least not yet. He had chosen to let the men grumble and mutter, thinking they might blow off steam. That night, however, he sensed that even his top officers were beginning to doubt him. They were better-trained and worthier seamen than the others, but Columbus began to fear that even the loyalty to command that is the supreme law of the sea would hold them for only so long.

For a moment, Columbus was able to put himself in their place and understand their point of view. Why should they believe in him? No one else had. Hadn't the mightiest monarchs of Europe been reluctant to fund his voyage? Hadn't the most powerful minds of the age said it was impossible? He had been told the distance was too far, that he wouldn't be able to carry enough supplies, that the Ocean Sea was unnavigable that far west. Even his friends laughed at his obsession, telling him to give up his dream and get on with his life. Everyone already knew he was a fine sailor, they said, and no one wants to hear about the western route to the Indies. Why couldn't he be satisfied simply to grow rich in the sea trade with the Canaries and Azores?

Columbus had dismissed his critics' arguments. They lacked imagination, he told himself. All of them — the nobles, the theologians, the other ships' captains who'd laughed at him — were timid and cautious, he felt. Their scorn fired his ambition. Riches? They were fools. Didn't they know that in the Orient there would be enough gold to fill the holds of one thousand ships? Didn't they know that a man could make ten fortunes trading in the silk, cinnamon, cotton, and jade that could be found there? Didn't they think that any monarch would reward the man who found the legendary passageway to the East? Why, he would be the most famous man in Christendom, and perhaps the wealthiest. No, Columbus couldn't blame his sailors for being among the skeptics. Better men than they had doubted him.

Still, Columbus knew that he would have to act soon to quell the incipient uprising. Every day the men grew more uneasy, more outspoken in their discontent. But if they thought they could frighten Columbus, they were mistaken. The trials he had endured to reach this point had only strengthened his determination. Even if the entire crew were to descend on him at once, brandishing weapons and demanding that they turn back, Columbus knew that he would insist on continuing the voyage. His crew would have to pitch him into the sea to get him to stop. The real challenge was to pick the right time and appropriate action to extinguish the mutiny before it gained momentum. The crew could not feel that they were being criticized or treated unfairly, for that would only inflame their resentment. Columbus had to bolster their spirits, make them see that they were engaged in a glorious adventure.

All these thoughts filled Columbus's head as he stood on the deck above his cabin. Normally a busy place, the deck was quiet now. Here and there Columbus spied what appeared to be large bundles scattered randomly about. These were sailors trying to seize a few minutes' sleep; only Columbus and the commanders of the other two ships had cabins or bunks. Along the deck rails other men gathered together to talk quietly or stare silently out to sea. Columbus wished he could hear what they were saying, but the wind carried their words away.

A few moments later, a ship's boy sounded the bells signifying midnight and the change of watch. Columbus looked on as two shapes rose and made their way aft. The two men took up a position at the rail a few feet away from Columbus. They had their backs to him and began to speak, oblivious of his presence.

"He's mad, you know," the first man said. "I've seen it before. He's got that faraway gleam in his eyes."

"Who?" the second man said. He had a hooked nose like a parrot's.

"The captain general." This was Columbus's official title.

"You really think he's crazy?" Parrot Beak asked.

"There's good reason why no one's ever sailed to Asia, you know. It can't be done. What does this Columbus fellow look like?"

"You serve under him as surely as I do," Parrot Beak replied, not quite understanding the question. "He looks much like any other man. Average height, blue eyes, white hair. Clean shaven when we began the journey."

"And his manner?" Diego asked.

"What are these questions? You know him as well as I do." "Answer me."

"Not outstanding, in any way. Rarely raises his voice. Refuses to swear; he uses no oaths stronger than 'by Saint Ferdinand.' Rather easygoing, I would say, compared to some captains I've known. Vigilant, however."

"His intelligence?"

"Well, he can read, which is more than you or I can do. But it seems only to have filled his head with outlandish notions."

"Don't you see?" Diego asked. He'd grown more animated and louder as the conversation progressed. "Does he seem remarkable to you in any way?"

"Only in that he believes the earth to be round, and that you can sail to the Orient. But they say that all educated people know that the earth is round," he replied, proud that he knew enough not to subscribe to the outdated notion that the earth was flat. He knew that many of his fellow sailors believed this to be true.

"And what about the first proposition?" Diego asked. He practically shouted the question. "Does it make sense that this man, who you concede is not remarkable in any way, should succeed where no one else has? Does it?" He'd grasped the unfortunate Parrot Beak by the shoulders and was shaking him violently.

"Well, he is devout," Parrot Beak whimpered. "After he leads the morning prayers and hymns on deck each morning, he retires to his cabin for private prayer. His cabin boy told me as much."

"Can his faith move continents?" Diego roared. "If all the learned geographers say Asia is ten thousand miles to the west, will Columbus's prayers move it farther east? Do you think the knowledge possessed by this Genoese is really greater than the wisdom of the ages? He doesn't even speak our language properly."

Columbus had listened unemotionally up to this point, but this last statement made him angry. He was proud of his Spanish. Columbus had been born in Genoa, Italy, and had grown up speaking Italian. He had taught himself Spanish.

"He has an accent, but he speaks passably enough," Parrot Beak replied. Columbus felt kindlier toward this sailor.

"Did your friend the cabin boy tell you about the phony log?" Diego asked. "Did he tell you that Columbus keeps two sets of figures, one for himself and one for the rest of us? According to his real log, which only our captain general sees, we've already sailed 2,700 miles west. If Columbus was right, we should have hit Asia 300 miles ago."

"How do you know?" Parrot Beak said quietly. "Francisco saw both journals. He sneaked into the captain general's cabin."

Columbus was stunned. This was an unforgivable breach of discipline. More important, should the news spread, the already disgruntled men were likely to panic. Mutiny would become a certainty.

Columbus stomped off and shook awake a ship's boy who was sleeping soundly. "Sound the All Hands" he bellowed. "God take you!" he thundered when the sleepy boy did not move fast enough to suit him. As the bells rang out, Columbus waited at the foremast for his crew to assemble.

It was a somewhat motley group that gathered before him. The men were dressed in a variety of different-colored tunics and breeches. Heavy boots covered their feet. Most of them worked and slept in the same set of clothing. And since few carried even one change of clothes with them, by this point in the journey, many of their outfits needed cleaning or repair. The men themselves looked shaggier than they did on shore. Believing that cutting one's hair on board brought bad luck, they had let it grow. They did not shave either, for the same reason, or cut their fingernails. In the flickering glow cast by the deck lanterns they appeared to be a rough and untamed lot.

There were thirty nine men aboard the *Santa María,* including Columbus. All but the helmsman gathered around the foremast. Columbus began to speak to them in a voice so low that some of the men in back had to press forward in order to hear.

"I am aware that you are unhappy," he began. "We are in strange waters, far away from home. We are bound for strange lands, which none of us has been to. That you should doubt is natural. But remember your duties. You are loyal subjects of King Ferdinand and Queen Isabella, to whom you have sworn obedience. I, too, am their sworn servant. I have been commissioned by them as Admiral of the Ocean Sea, and as Viceroy and Governor of all lands that we discover. I carry their letter of greeting, embossed with the royal seal, to the Great Khan of China. On board this ship, indeed until we land once again on Spanish shores, I am the Crown."

A murmuring began among the men. "We will never see Spain again," one of them shouted angrily. "The wind has been at our back the entire time." A prevalence of rear wind was held by superstitious sailors to be a bad omen.

"Think what you say," Columbus said calmly. "How can that wind which speeds you toward your destination be an evil harbinger? Look above you. The sky has been clear each night. Rarely have you seen such an untroubled sky. If heaven disapproved of our mission, surely it would be registered in the stars." Columbus was referring to the widely held belief that meteor showers, shooting stars, comets, and other astronomical phenomena were signs of heavenly disfavor.

"I was speaking in earthly, not heavenly, terms," the same sailor responded. "If the wind is behind us now, what will power us on our return journey?" A few men voiced their support of this sailor's logic.

"We will return at a higher latitude," Columbus said. "We first sailed south to the Canaries because my observation on earlier voyages told me that westerly winds blow on that line."

The sailor stood quieted. "I hear things at night," one of his colleagues called out in a panicky voice. "Like the ghosts of sailors who've perished on this route before us."

"What you hear is the wind in the sails, and the hull creaking, and the supplies shifting," said Columbus scornfully. "No one has preceded us here, so there can be no ghosts.

"You are fearful, like children," Columbus continued. "The Lord rewards those who are bold in their faith. Do you not think He will favor those who seek to bring the true faith to the Indies? Do you not think He will bless with riches those who bring His gospel to the Orient? Think of your scripture, in which Jesus tells the multitudes to remember the birds of the sky, who neither plant nor harvest crops, yet the Heavenly Father feeds them. Do you not think he will do the same for you? Jesus asks them. And is there one man among you who does not think that the Lord is watching over him at this moment? How can you doubt that our mission is destined for success? We've received fine weather, and the prevailing winds have favored us. 'Seek, and ye shall find,' the Bible tells us. I am at peace with my god, and he assures me that my mission will succeed. I entreat you to share my confidence.

You have all heard the name Marco Polo, have you not? Do you not realize that each man who participates in this voyage will someday be as famous as Polo? Do you not think that Ferdinand and Isabella will handsomely reward each of their faithful servants who helps claim the Orient for them? Already they have promised a year's pay to the first sailor to sight land. Each of you has heard of the wealth Polo discovered in the Orient. What do you think awaits us? Why, each of you will be nobles in the new lands that lie before you, and your wives and children will live on great estates! You will wear doublets lined with jewels and ride only the finest horses! Asia is not far off. I have studied the charts; I know it is near. Ahead of you lies an opportunity offered only a few men, if only you have the faith to take it. Be bold; trust in your faith. It is useless to complain. I have come this far to go to the Indies, and I cannot stop until, with the Lord's help, I find them."

With that he dismissed the crew. The men dispersed in silence, but once out of the captain general's earshot they talked excitedly of the one year's bonus that was being offered for sighting land. Exactly one week later, early in the morning of October 12, 1492, Rodrigo de Triana, a lookout on the *Pinta,* shouted, "Land ho!" The cry rang out across the water, and the crews of all three ships, including Columbus, rushed to the rail for a glimpse of what lay ahead.

As Columbus stared at the shoreline, he found his mind racing backward. The dream that he had had was now reality.

2

In Love with the Sea

CHRISTOPHER COLUMBUS WAS born in the port city of Genoa, Italy, sometime between August 25 and the end of October 1451. In Italian, the language spoken by the inhabitants of Genoa, his name was Cristoforo Colombo. As was customary, his parents had given their son the name of a saint of the Catholic Church, Saint Christopher. It was believed that Saint Christopher had carried the Christ child across a dangerous river; Saint Christopher has since been thought of as the patron saint of travelers.

The boy's father was Domenico Colombo, a respected wool weaver and officer in the local guild, or trade union. His mother, Susanna Fontanarossa, was the daughter of a wool weaver. Christopher was their first child. He would be followed by at least three brothers and a sister. Two of the brothers — Bartholomew and Giacomo, who is always referred to by the Spanish equivalent of his name, Diego — would sail with Christopher to the New World.

At the time of Columbus's birth, Genoa was an independent city, located in what is now northwest Italy, on the Ligurian Sea. Italy did not yet exist as a united nation; it consisted instead of a number of principalities, duchies, and, in the north, independent city-states. Genoa had for some time been the proudest and strongest of these city-states, famous for its ship captains, sailors, and shipbuilders. From its bustling harbor its expert seamen sailed off in all directions to bring back trade goods to "that noble and powerful city of the sea," as Columbus later called his birthplace.

The family had a long tradition in the wool trade, and Domenico's business enjoyed a certain amount of success. He owned his own looms and at times employed as many as half a dozen journeymen to spin the wool into finished cloth. However, this measure of accomplishment did not seem to be enough for his wife, Susanna, who complained that there was never enough money. This meant that the Columbus household was frequently filled with the sounds of shouting and fighting. And there was some truth to Susanna's complaints: She had many mouths to feed, and although Domenico was hardly irresponsible, at times he could be less than diligent. Possessing a friendly, congenial temperament, he was not given to worrying, and he believed that what could not be done today could be done tomorrow. It broke his heart to be indoors on a sunny day, and he thought nothing of closing down the shop, gathering up his oldest boy and a couple of his cronies, and heading off for a day of that favorite Genoese pastime — fishing. Domenico also enjoyed a glass or two at the local tavern, and he did not hesitate when it was his turn to buy a round of drinks.

The young Christopher loved both of his parents, and was disturbed by the domestic conflict. A quiet, sensitive child, he escaped from the unpleasant atmosphere at home by taking long walks along the waterfront. The burly stevedores, rakish sailors, and harried merchants there soon grew accustomed to the sight of the small, shy, red-haired child taking in the hustle and bustle of the harbor with his bright blue eyes. Mostly they were too busy to stop and talk with him, but he was a well-behaved boy, and they did not mind his watching. Some even kept an eye on him to see that none of the waterfront's notorious thieves gave him any trouble.

From the time of his first visit to the harbor the young Columbus felt that he belonged there. Many boys would have been frightened by the coarse behavior of the sailors, and by their colorful tattoos. Columbus, however, was fascinated. He loved to listen as the merchants' clerks sounded off the items that the stevedores, grunting and sweating under their load, carried from the holds of the ships. There were barrels of Madeira wine, vats of dyes, chests of silk and wool, and barrels of exotic spices such as cinnamon, nutmeg, cloves, ginger, vanilla, saffron, and Malabar pepper. Incense, perfume, and sugar were mentioned, along with precious gems and metals such as gold, silver, and rubies. The ships, with their tall masts, ivory-colored sails, intricate riggings, and carved wooden hulls, made a deep impression on the young Columbus. The names of the ships' destinations fired the young boy's imagination: Ireland and England, Castile and Aragon, the Canary Islands, the Gold Coast of Africa, the Azores, Chios and Crete, Tunis, Morocco, and the Levant.

Although unschooled, Columbus was a bright child, and it did not take long for him to make sense of what he saw and heard. The most important trade items — spices, perfume, sugar, precious metals, and gems — came from the Levant, those lands bordering the eastern Mediterranean Sea between Greece and Egypt. However, these goods did not originate in the Levant. They'd come by caravan, over mountains and across rivers and deserts, from a more distant area to the east known as the Indies or the Orient. These were the lands that Marco Polo, a young man from Venice, another Italian city-state and Genoa's great commercial rival, had visited almost two centuries earlier. Marco Polo had been one of the first Europeans to visit those fabled places. He had returned to Venice with what seemed to be outlandish tales of a mighty ruler known as the Great Khan and palaces roofed with gold.

The treasures Columbus saw pouring out of the ship holds day after day seemed to prove that Polo had told the truth. It had not taken long for the geographers and ships' captains to determine that great wealth could be amassed if a route to sail to the Indies was discovered. Because the Indies lay to the east, it was thought that the most logical route was to sail south, around the tip of Africa, and then on to the Orient. The first Genoese attempt to make the voyage had occurred in 1291 but had failed. A similar fate had befallen all efforts since.

By the 1450s, the need to find a sea route to the Indies had taken on a new urgency for Genoese captains and merchants. Transporting goods overland from Asia to the port cities of the Levant had become difficult and dangerous. Caravans were waylaid by bandits and plunderers, and the travelers themselves suffered from the desert heat, sandstorms, disease, and other hazards. This made the cost of those goods that did arrive extremely high. In addition, the Ottoman Turks had been expanding their empire to include the coastal regions of the Levant. The Turks were Muslims, and they showed less inclination to trade with the Christians of Europe than had their Christian predecessors in the Levant. Although Venice was enjoying increased success in trading with the Levant, Genoese commerce there was declining. All these reasons made it important that an alternate route to the Indies be discovered. Several Genoese captains set forth on such a quest during Columbus's childhood, but they all returned home disappointed and frustrated. Uncooperative weather, frightened crews, and a shortage of supplies frustrated all those who had attempted to make the unprecedented journey.

Over time the sea came to dominate Columbus's imagination, his soul, and finally his entire being. Only the church occupied a similar place in his thoughts. From his earliest days, Columbus possessed a deep religious faith. Although he could neither read nor write, he was able to memorize many prayers, hymns, and Biblical passages. The mysteries of the Catholic faith excited his imagination almost as much as the sea and its horizons. He attended Mass regularly, said his morning and evening prayers each day without fail, and like many a youth before and after him believed that God had singled him out for something special, some great deed for which he would long be remembered.

Domenico and Susanna did not discourage their eldest son's interest in the sea. Columbus spent most of his days working a loom in his father's shop, but Domenico recognized signs of his son's restlessness. In 1461, when Columbus was ten, Domenico allowed him to go to sea for the first time. These first voyages were little more than short trips with trusted friends of Domenico's, taken to deliver some woolen goods or other items to a neighboring city. To Columbus, however, they were grand adventures. The sea was just as he had imagined it would be. The breezes ruffled his hair, and the salt air invigorated him as it filled his lungs. Once at sea a tremendous feeling of solitude, both frightening and exhilarating, took hold of him. The earth seemed to drop away and the ship found itself surrounded by water and sky. It was a moment to trust in oneself and in one's God. There was so much to learn! The observant little boy involved himself in every aspect of life on board ship. What he couldn't figure out through watching he asked about. Few of his fellow sailors were ever too busy to answer the questions of the curious redhead.

By the time Columbus was fifteen he was making longer journeys, some lasting a month or more, to various ports along the Mediterranean. All those with whom he sailed were impressed by his abilities, his willingness to work hard, and his eagerness to learn more. In between voyages he continued to labor in his father's shop, but Domenico realized that Christopher would not be the son to succeed him in the wool trade. That was too bad, Domenico thought. The boy was bright, and he was already far more ambitious than his father had ever been. Christopher had spoken to his father many times of his intention to gain wealth and fame. With such drive he would surely have made the family business extremely successful, Domenico thought sadly. However, it was plain to see that his son's desire for fame and fortune was tied to an unalterable determination to see foreign lands. The boy thought of little else but the sea.

As his hunger for adventure grew stronger, Columbus spent less and less time in Domenico's shop. In 1470, when he was nineteen, he served as a sailor in the fleet formed by René II, the king of the French province of Anjou. Anjou was at war with the Spanish province of Aragon. However, Columbus's ship saw no action. Six years later, in May 1476, Columbus shipped out from the port of Genoa aboard a Flemish vessel known as the *Bechalla*. The *Bechalla* was one of several armed vessels chartered by Genoese merchants to protect an extremely valuable cargo of goods that was being sent to ports in northern Europe.

The first part of the journey, west across the Mediterranean, was uneventful. Being at sea (and out of Domenico's shop) thrilled Columbus, although in truth he was just the least bit restless during this early leg of the journey. Columbus's seafaring had thus far been confined to the Mediterranean. He was eager to journey farther and see more. This trip held the promise of both: The itinerary included France, Flanders, Holland, England, and maybe Germany and Denmark to the far north. Perhaps he would even find the time and money to get to Lisbon, Portugal, where his younger brother Bartholomew was living.

The desire to see Bartholomew was not the only reason Columbus had for wanting to visit Lisbon. Lisbon was the largest port and most important city in the country of Portugal. Backed by monarchs eager for wealth and conquest, Portuguese sailors roamed far and wide on the seas in search of new lands and trade routes. Their discoveries had made Portugal the wealthiest and most powerful nation in Europe, and sailors from across the continent, including those from Genoa, were eager to go there.

As a succession of calm, windless days slowed the *Bechalla's* progress, Columbus began to think about how he could improve his station in life. He had long since mastered the routine duties he was expected to perform. He had no doubt that a seamen's life was grand, and was surely to be preferred to life ashore. Beyond that, though, Columbus believed he was destined for greatness. He wanted a command of his own. But to obtain a command required both money and connections. He had neither, but figured that Lisbon was a near-perfect place to look for both.

At last the *Bechalla* passed through the Strait of Gibraltar and on into the Atlantic Ocean, although neither Columbus nor any of his shipmates knew it as such. Like even the most learned geographers and cartographers (mapmakers) of the day, Columbus believed that all the earth's oceans were a single body of water, known as the Ocean Sea.

The Genoese merchants had acted wisely in taking steps to secure protection for their merchandise. On the morning of August 13, 1476, as the Genoese convoy passed along the southern coast of Portugal, it was set upon by a French fleet bent on plunder. Columbus was not surprised by the attack. Piracy, often conducted by ships and crews operating with the sanction of their government, occurred quite frequently on the high seas. What did impress Columbus, as he watched from his vantage point on the deck of the *Bechalla,* was the maneuverability of the French vessels. The French were not renowned as sailors or shipbuilders, yet their fleet appeared to be quicker and more responsive than the Genoese convoy. The French ships moved speedily to separate the Genoese ships from one another, like predators cutting off their prey from the herd.

Cannon fire began to hit the decks of the Genoese vessels, and a series of well-placed blasts shredded the sails and toppled the foremast of the *Bechalla*. The Genoese answered with cannon fire, and Columbus joined in the cheers as the *Bechalla*'s first shots hit home. Fierce fighting followed, and at times the smoke from the cannons and primitive muskets was so thick that Columbus could not see more than ten feet in front of him on deck. The French vessel's hull rammed the *Bechalla*'s as it swung in close enough for its crew to attempt a boarding. Its masts loomed out of the gunpowder haze, looking like a ghost vessel.

Columbus's own actions seemed dreamlike and automatic; he operated on instinct. When the battle was over he would be hard-pressed to say exactly what it was he had done during those frantic hours. Yet the cries of the combatants sounded all too real to Columbus, as did the whistle of the musket balls, the crash of iron shot colliding with wood, and the clang of sword against sword. Immersed in the fighting, Columbus scarcely noticed that the sun had passed its meridian and was sinking toward the western horizon. Indeed, drenched in sweat, filthy and exhausted, he would have been unable to say whether the battle had been fought under sunny or overcast skies. As nightfall approached,

Columbus had even forgotten that he'd been wounded by shrapnel from a French cannon shot. He had been wounded in his neck and shoulder, and his tunic was drenched in blood.

As the darkness descended a final French cannonade tore into the already badly damaged *Bechalla*. The ship had been taking on water for hours and this last fusillade finished it off. The *Bechalla* sank rapidly. Interested in booty rather than captives, the French trusted that the sea would finish off their work for them. They made no effort to save those sailors who were still alive. After silently saying his prayers, Columbus leapt from the deck of the sinking wreck into the dark waters of the war-torn Ocean Sea. Columbus had been a powerful swimmer since boyhood, so he had no trouble keeping himself afloat, but his shoulder pained him and he doubted whether he would be able to swim very far. In the distance a ship burned brightly. He could not tell whether it was French or Genoese. Occasionally, Columbus heard the cry of a wounded or dying man, but aside from that the night had grown quiet. The sea, too, had calmed itself, as if it had expunged all evidence of the man-made tempest that such a brief time ago had disturbed its waters. The French attacker of the *Bechalla* had moved away in the general direction of the burning vessel, and the *Bechalla* itself was now beneath the waves.

Columbus watched and listened for signs that any of his shipmates had survived, but he detected nothing. He was surprised to notice that there were stars in the sky, but he felt indifferent to their charm, too indifferent even to pray. For a brief moment Columbus thought about how easy it would be to stop swimming and sink beneath the water while the stars winked out, one by one, above him. His shoulder ached, and he was exhausted. But then he noticed a sweep — a long-handled wooden oar — floating in the water a few yards to his right. Columbus roused himself from his despair, swam to it, and grabbed on. The sweep would keep him afloat; all he had to do was cling to it and kick. Columbus looked around and tried to figure out which way was north. Then he mouthed a simple and heartfelt prayer — "Thank you, Lord" — and headed in the direction of what he hoped was Portugal.

3

Pleading His Case

THE NIGHT SEEMED endless. Columbus drifted for hours, uncertain of how far he was from land or whether he was even moving in the right direction. At times he lost consciousness, awakening only when a wave splashed over his head. While it seemed to Columbus as if he must have slept for hours, in truth these blackouts lasted no more than a moment or so.

During these spells of unconsciousness, vivid dreamlike images flashed through his mind. He saw his mother and father smiling and dressed in their Sunday finery. He saw the dark and battered hull of the *Bechalla* just before it slid beneath the waters. He saw the small stone church in the mountains north of Genoa where he had attended Mass before leaving on this voyage. He heard the strange-sounding war cries of the French and a church choir singing beautiful, exalted hymns.

Each time Columbus returned to consciousness he became discouraged. He could not be sure how long he had slept, and with no markers to guide him he could not tell whether he was getting any closer to land. Though Columbus was a skilled sailor, and knew how to navigate by the stars, his ordeal had left him disoriented. That night the stars seemed as strange and incomprehensible to him as a foreign language. He was mad at himself, too, for having considered giving up and allowing himself to drown beneath the waves. One should not give in so easily, he told himself, no matter how hopeless a situation appears to be. Surely, he thought with certainty, this was not the fate the Lord had marked for him.

Soon the sky began to lighten, and Columbus thought he could detect a faint, pinkish glow on the horizon. That must be the sunrise, he thought. If so, I'm heading north, and Portugal must lie ahead. Columbus kicked his feet for the first time in almost an hour and moved forward. But dawn comes slowest for those who await it, and Columbus began to fear that he'd only imagined the glow on the horizon. Perhaps, he thought, it was only a light trick — starlight glinting off the water, or the glow from the burning ship he'd left behind. Columbus wondered whether he'd become delirious, whether hallucinations had taken over his normally rational mind. He thought he might be dreaming and would soon awaken to find himself gasping for breath from a wave breaking over him. But then the sky brightened in earnest and revealed waves crashing onto a rock-strewn beach. Columbus soon found himself washed ashore. He had reached Lagos, a fishing village on Portugal's southern coast.

Too exhausted to move, he lay on the beach for several hours before being discovered by some local fishermen. One of them took Columbus home, offered him clothes and food, and nursed the ship-wrecked sailor back to health over the course of several weeks. In return, Columbus helped by mending the fisherman's netting and equipment. When his strength returned, Columbus lent a hand on the fisherman's boat.

All in all, it turned into a pleasant convalescence, but now that Providence had seen fit to deliver him to Portugal, Columbus did not intend to tarry long in the small village of Lagos. Lisbon was the place for a sailor and prospective captain, and Columbus intended to get there. After a couple of months Columbus arranged to ship out with a merchant who had goods to deliver to Lisbon. Columbus said good-bye to his benefactor and set sail for the Portuguese capital.

Columbus's first sight of Lisbon was everything he expected it to be. He marveled as his ship made its way up the river and past the miles of docks that lined the banks of the river that led up to the city. And the port! Columbus had never seen anything so grand. Galleons and caravels vied for space with smaller fishing boats. Judging from the multitude of brightly colored flags and pennants — all bearing coats of arms — that festooned the tall sails and flapped and fluttered in the light breeze, it seemed

29

as if every monarch, prince, and duke in Europe had sent ships to Lisbon. Also in port were the ships of countless individual entrepreneurs. Many vessels flew the insignias of the guilds and mercantile leagues that owned or sponsored them. Columbus's ship sailed close enough for him to see the enormous warehouses that sprawled out onto the wharfs and docks. He saw the countinghouses where merchants tallied the profits from the latest shipment from the Gold Coast of Africa and beyond. Rowboats paddled from shore to ship, bearing traders who welcomed the returned captains, examined their loot, and arranged for future voyages.

At last Lisbon itself came into view, crowded and beautiful. Like Rome, it was built on seven hills, and its skyline dominated the horizon. It seemed a study in pastel. Most of the buildings were white or pink; here and there a pale blue or green structure shone through. Tall towers and steeples towered over the slate roofs of the houses and commercial buildings. East of the teeming business section, which ran down to the waterfront, Columbus was able to pick out the Alfama district, with its steep, narrow streets and twisting thoroughfares. He saw the castle of Saint George, home to the Portuguese monarchs. Columbus knew that it was from the Castle of Saint George that Prince Henry the Navigator had sent his mariners in search of riches and the eastern route to the Indies. One day, Columbus thought, some enlightened monarch would send him on a similarly important mission.

Columbus was so eager to begin his exploration of Lisbon and to find his brother Bartholomew that he almost forgot to collect his wages before leaving the ship. Finding Bartholomew proved easy; he was employed in one of the chart-making establishments near the waterfront. He got a job there for Christopher. Before long the two brothers had a thriving practice of their own. More important, it kept Columbus in touch with developments in Lisbon's seagoing community. Chart making was a good, profitable business. The most successful chart makers were those whose charts contained the most up-to-date news on trade routes and discoveries. This information could only be obtained from the captains returning from their latest voyages. Columbus thus found himself among the crowds that lined the waterfront awaiting the return of voyagers to Africa and other points. He would buttonhole the captain and his chief officers, inviting them to dine with him and his brother. During dinner, he and Bartholomew would question the mariners about their observations and experiences. Then the two brothers would spend the next several days drawing up maps based on what they had learned. Their contacts and expertise made the Columbus brothers respected chartmakers. Columbus, however, had more in mind than the new family business as he listened to the sailors' tales. He planned on returning to sea, this time as a captain. He listened in order to learn things that would help him achieve fame.

An idea had begun to form in Columbus's head, an audacious and brilliant concept. And yet his reasoning was rather simple: All trade with the Far East was controlled by the Muslims, for it was they who controlled the important overland routes with China and India. This meant that the path to direct trade with China and India was barred to Europeans. But what if one sailed to the west? figured Columbus. If the world was round, as many people claimed, then it might be possible to circle the world and reach the two great lands by sailing west!

Columbus realized that he needed to know more in order to bring such a plan to fruition. It was no easy task to persuade kings and queens to fund an expedition that had never been attempted before. One had to demonstrate expertise; one had to be familiar with the knowledge and wisdom of the age. And though Columbus was bright — he had learned Portuguese with little trouble — he was illiterate. His first step, then, was to teach himself to read, which he did with painstaking effort. The effort awoke in him a passion for learning, and he soon amassed a sizeable library, covering the margins of the books he read with detailed and intricate notes. He taught himself Latin, which enabled him to read the Bible and voluminous geographical treatises. Soon Columbus was spending almost all his spare time poring over his books on geography.

The more Columbus read, the more excited he became. If the world was indeed a sphere, as all scholars claimed it to be, then it should be possible to sail west to reach the East. In other words, a ship could set sail due west from Lisbon, across the Ocean Sea, and land in Cipangu, the islands we know today as Japan, or in China. The idea that the earth was flat, and that those who sailed too far might topple off the edge, had long since been discredited. Only uneducated and superstitious people believed that was true. Educated people all believed that the earth was spherical in shape.

Columbus reasoned that his plan must be feasible. He knew from his reading that the ancient Greeks had determined that a sphere could be divided into 360 degrees. If one knew how long a degree was, then it would be simple to determine the distance across the Ocean Sea that separated Europe from China. Columbus had studied Ptolemy's Geography, the work of a second-century Greek mathematician and geographer who lived in Alexandria, Egypt, one of the ancient world's great seats of learning. Ptolemy, whose work was regarded as definitive by most Europeans, estimated a degree at fifty nautical miles. Columbus had other ideas. He had read the work of Alfragan, a ninth-century Muslim geographer who, Columbus thought, had written that a degree equaled forty-five nautical miles. Columbus chose to believe Alfragan, rather than Ptolemy. In fact, Columbus had misinterpreted Alfragan. The Muslim had believed a degree to be sixty-six nautical miles, an assertion much closer to today's estimate. Today we know that a degree equals sixty nautical miles.

Once Columbus had established that measurement to his own satisfaction, he needed to figure the total land mass, in degrees, of Europe and Asia. Again, he had several sources to choose from. Ptolemy believed that the two continents occupied 180 degrees. Columbus again disregarded Ptolemy's work. Marinus of Tyre, a Levantine geographer whose work predated Ptolemy's, put the figure at 225 degrees. Columbus preferred that figure and used it as the basis of his calculations.

It is clear why Columbus preferred Marinus's figure. If Marinus's hypothesis were true, the journey across the Ocean Sea was shorter. It was for this same reason that Columbus chose the shorter estimate of the length of a degree. According to Columbus, less than sixty degrees separated the two continents, a distance he calculated at 2,400 miles.

Columbus's idea came to obsess him. He spoke of it to all who would listen. Why this fascination with sailing around the tip of Africa to reach Asia, he asked, when it would be safer and shorter to sail due west? Within a short time, people learned not to argue with Columbus on this point, for he would not be swayed. Indeed, his conviction was so great that he began to earn a reputation as a crank. He could not help himself, though. His reading and studies all seemed to verify his conclusions. He even found support for his ideas in the Bible. In the Second Book of Esdras, a part of the Apocrypha to the Old Testament, there is a line that reads, "Six parts hast thou dried up." According to Columbus, these words meant that since six-sevenths of the earth was land, only one-seventh could be ocean. In his copy of the play *Medea*, by Euripedes, the Greek dramatist, Columbus underscored this phrase several times: "A time will come when the chains of the Ocean will fall apart, and a vast continent be revealed; when a pilot will discover new worlds . . ."

Those who disagreed with Columbus were treated to quotations and allusions from the Greek philosopher Aristotle, the Greek geographer Strabo, and Columbus's favorite, the French geographer Pierre D'Ailly, author of *Imago Mundi.* A copy of this last work was always by Columbus's bedside. Ever since his childhood, Columbus had believed that God had ordained special things for him. He was now convinced that it was his destiny to discover a new route to the Indies.

In fact, little about Columbus's idea was new. Many people had had the same idea. What set Columbus apart from these others was the depth of his conviction and his tenacity. Mariners had discussed the idea of sailing west for centuries, but none had seriously pursued the idea. There were stories of sailors who had tried, but these were shrouded in myth and legend. Few Europeans had heard of Leif Ericson, the Viking sailor who supposedly discovered a new land somewhere to the west around the year 1000. Today we believe that the land the Vikings discovered was either New England or Nova Scotia, Canada. Somewhat more familiar to Portuguese mariners, because of their trade journeys to Ireland, was the legend of Saint Brendan, the sixth-century Irish monk who claimed to have landed on islands in the west after a journey of thousands of miles in a small boat. Portuguese sailors were also fond of speaking of Antilia, an island said to be located somewhere in the middle of the Ocean Sea. Antilia was allegedly inhabited by refugees from Portugal's earlier wars with the Moors, Arab Muslims who had conquered much of southern Spain in the eighth century. Indeed, there were many who believed that what Columbus proposed was possible in theory. What made Columbus special was his unyielding determination to make his dream a reality.

That determination was to prove Columbus's greatest asset, since virtually all of his calculations were to prove to be spectacularly wrongheaded. Both Ptolemy and Alfragan were closer in their estimate of the length of a degree than Columbus, meaning that Columbus had underestimated the actual size of the earth by 25 percent. The combined length of Europe and Asia is only 130 degrees, and Japan is actually a total of 10,600 miles from the Canary Islands.

Many years would pass before Columbus would have an opportunity to test his figures. While a part of him was a dreamer, the other part was a hardheaded realist. Columbus knew that no chart maker, no matter how well regarded, could expect to persuade a wealthy patron to provide him with the men, money, ships, and equipment needed for a risky journey of discovery. Columbus had no reputation in Lisbon as a seaman; he would have to prove himself as a sailor under the Portuguese flag before he could ask that nation's king to support him.

In the fall of 1476 Columbus sailed on a Portuguese vessel that carried wool, fish, and wine to the Azores, Ireland, and Iceland. At the Irish port of Galway, Columbus and his shipmates were astonished by the discovery of two corpses, a man and a woman, adrift in a boat. Neither Columbus nor any of the Portuguese had ever seen humans of such extraordinary appearance. The Irish said that they were Chinese. In all likelihood the dead people were Lapps or Eskimos, but the sighting seemed further proof to Columbus that China could not be all that far away. Columbus made several similar trading journeys over the next several years, but on the whole seemed no closer to reaching his goal of leading a voyage to the Far East.

Columbus's personal life was more eventful. In 1479 he was introduced to Dona Felipa Perestrello e moniz, a demure, dark-haired beauty he had noticed many times in church. The two got along well from the start. Columbus's interest increased when he learned that Dona Felipa belonged to one of Portugal's finest families — one that even possessed impeccable seagoing credentials. Her grandfather had been a knight and close adviser to Henry the Navigator, and her late father, Bartholomew Perestrello, had been a captain in the Portuguese merchant marine. The father had discovered the island of Porto Santo, in the Madeira Island group, and had been awarded its hereditary governorship.

Columbus and Dona Felipa fell deeply in love. Columbus had little to recommend himself as a suitor to a woman with such prestigious ancestors. He could offer neither riches, a noble family name, nor the guarantee of a bright future. But Dona Felipa's mother was impressed by his ambition, and the family accepted his marriage proposal. The couple married late in 1479 and moved in with Dona Felipa's mother, who gave her late husband's logbooks and charts to her new son-in-law. A year later Columbus and his bride moved to Porto Santo, where Dona Felipa gave birth to their only child, Diego. In 1482 they settled on Funchal, another of the Madeira islands. His in-laws' connections soon proved beneficial to his career. In Funchal Columbus received his first command — over a caravel headed for a trading post on Africa's Gold Coast.

At one time in his life a command of his own had been Columbus's only dream, but now he dreamed of greater conquests, such as finding a western route to the riches of the East. On a trip to the Azores he claimed to have seen a natural rock formation in the shape of a horseman pointing west. Columbus took this as an omen of his destiny to discover the western route to the Indies.

With his skills and family connections, there is little doubt that Columbus could have made a comfortable, even prosperous, living as a captain in the Portuguese merchant marine. The African trade offered an opportunistic captain countless opportunities to enrich himself. After a time, the king might even give him the opportunity to explore the farther reaches of the African coast, past the last Portuguese trading post, or to attempt the eastward passage to the Indies. Columbus, however, had his own ideas about reaching the East. He was certain that the wealth he would find in the East would make the riches of the Gold Coast seem a mere pittance. Marco Polo, Alfragan, Ptolemy, and all the rest would be forgotten — he, Columbus, would be remembered for all time.

4

Convincing the Confessor

EVENTUALLY, COLUMBUS REALIZED that it would be much easier for him to pursue his ambitions from the Portuguese capital. Upon his return from the voyage to the Gold Coast, he brought his family back to Lisbon, and in 1484 made his first attempt to attract a royal sponsor, the King of Portugal.

King John II of Portugal, a nephew of Henry the Navigator, listened as Columbus enthusiastically recited his proposal to sail to Japan and the East, but the monarch was unimpressed. According to a court historian: "The King, as he observed this *Christovao Colom to be a big talker and boastful* . . . and full of fancy and imagination with his Isle *Cypango* . . . gave him small credit." Nevertheless, the king did see enough in Columbus and his project to refer the idea to a committee of clergymen and two Jewish physicians for deliberation; the latter were experienced in celestial navigation. The churchmen and doctors were no more optimistic about Columbus's prospects for success than the king had been. They cited their own research to Columbus, telling him that the distance to Japan was certainly much greater than he believed it to be. No ship, no matter how well stocked, could carry enough supplies to make it, they said. Furthermore, beyond a certain point, the waters of the Ocean Sea became unnavigable.

Columbus and the king also differed on nonscientific issues. The king and his advisers were put off by Columbus's insistence that he be paid handsomely for his efforts. Columbus demanded a percentage of whatever riches he brought back for the king, and expected to be appointed governor of whatever new islands and lands he discovered en route to the East. Portuguese kings were unaccustomed to such requests. They expected their captains to undertake voyages in exchange for expenses only and to trust in the generosity of their monarch for a future reward should the voyage meet with success. The presumption of the upstart Genoan in demanding compensation was considered appalling.

Columbus was disappointed that King John did not have the foresight of his uncle, Henry the Navigator, but for the moment remained undaunted. That feeling of superiority left him a few months later when his wife, Dona Felipa, died after a brief illness. Along with his brother, Bartholomew, Dona Felipa had been one of the few people who believed in him unconditionally. Her death left him feeling heartbroken, isolated, and alone. Not even Bartholomew could console him.

Although Columbus possessed a seemingly unshakeable self-confidence in his abilities and destiny, he was prone on occasion to self-doubt and moments of despair. The combination of his wife's death and the Portuguese king's rejection plunged Columbus into a deep and profound depression. He told himself that he had been a fool to believe that he had a future in Portugal. Why did he stay? he asked himself. He had no friends there. There was not a man in the whole country farsighted enough to see the truth of his proposal. Even if such people existed, no one would support him now that the king had turned his proposal down. He thought it might be time to start anew. After all, John II wasn't the only monarch with a rich treasury.

Columbus decided that Spain was the logical place for him to go. Although Spain had no reputation as a naval power, exciting things were happening there. Its Catholic monarchs — *los reyes Catolicos* in the language of their own land — King Ferdinand and Queen Isabella, had by virtue of their marriage united the country's two most powerful regions, Castile and Aragon. They had defeated an army of Portuguese invaders. Currently they were trying to drive the Moors from their strongholds in the south. Columbus reasoned that the Catholic monarchs would jump at the opportunity to add to their power by claiming new lands in the Orient. He also reasoned that it would particularly

41

appeal to them to beat their Portuguese rivals to such a prize. Columbus imagined the consternation that would reign in the Portuguese court when King John II learned that Ferdinand and Isabella had funded the same voyage he had turned down. His confidence rekindled, Columbus decided that the recent calamities had been a test, the Lord's way of determining whether he was worthy of the great mission for which he had been selected. Columbus set out for Spain with a renewed sense of the greatness of his destiny.

His first glimpse of Spain could not have made him less optimistic. Palos, the small city where he landed, was by Lisbon's standards an insignificant backwater. No foreign vessels crowded its rundown quays, and the only ships leaving port on the day Columbus arrived were small fishing boats. Columbus's depression returned. He had no money, and, from a realistic point of view, no real prospects. How did he expect his proposal to reach the monarchs? He knew no one at court. He didn't even know where the court was located. Not even the Spanish seemed to know. Ferdinand and Isabella were traveling from city to city overseeing the war with the Moors, and no one seemed certain where the court would be called to convene next.

There was one positive omen. As his ship had made its way to Palos, he had noticed some dun-colored buildings on the bluff overlooking the river. He suspected that they might be home to a religious order, and inquiries in town confirmed his suspicions. The buildings were part of the friary known as La Rábida, where priests from the Franciscan order lived. Columbus had always liked the Franciscans. Like their founder, St. Francis of Assisi, they enjoyed a reputation for piety, austerity, simplicity, and charity. Perhaps they would take pity on an impoverished pilgrim and his tired and bedraggled five-year-old son.

Columbus and and his son, Diego, walked the four miles to the friary, hoping they would would not be turned away without a simple meal and perhaps the invitation to rest for a while. The good friars did not disappoint. Columbus and his son were met at the gate by Antonio de Marchena, a well-read, scholarly priest who was also a student of astronomy and navigation. Something about Columbus attracted the priest's attention. Perhaps it was the glint of conviction in his blue eyes, or the hint of intelligence in his halting and clumsy Spanish. Before long, the two men were discussing geography and the possibility of finding a northwest passage to the Orient.

Antonio de Marchena was impressed by Columbus. Although Columbus was obviously not of noble birth — he was in fact reticent about discussing his origins — he was devout and well read. He spoke Latin passably well and he was familiar with the Bible. It was, however, Columbus's convictions that Marchena found most exciting. He could see that Columbus was absolutely convinced that he had been selected by God to find a new route to the Indies, so much so that he referred to himself as an "emissary of the Holy Trinity." He would claim the

new lands he found for Spain, and would convert
the peoples he found there to Christianity. For
Marchena, who had long speculated on such possi-
bilities, their conversation was immensely exciting.

Columbus was equally impressed with the priest.
He had grown somewhat closemouthed about his
ambitions since his setbacks in Portugal, but in the
presence of a sympathetic listener his spirit re-
joiced. His speech reflected all the passion he felt for
his idea, all the frustrations he had encountered in
its pursuit, all the years of gentle mockery and chid-
ing he had endured. Like many an individual who
pursues a personal vision that isolates him or her
from others, Columbus was not without a touch of
self-pity.

The gentle and wise priest seemed to understand
Columbus, and he invited Columbus and Diego to
spend the night. More important, several days later
he introduced Columbus to the Count of Medina
Celi, a wealthy nobleman and shipowner who was
intensely interested in ocean exploration. Columbus, who rarely hesitated to press his advantages,
almost immediately asked Medina Celi for "three or
four well-equipped caravels, and no more," with
which he could undertake a voyage to the East. The
count was on the verge of complying when he realized that such an important undertaking needed to
be cleared with the Crown. He wrote to the queen,
who responded by summoning Columbus to her
court.

Columbus did not immediately respond to the
queen's invitation and thus missed the court's ses-

sion in Córdoba. By the time Columbus arrived, the queen and her retinue were gone. Because the Spanish court was still engaged in its travels and Columbus did not have enough money to follow, he went to Córdoba to await the court's arrival there. He made friends with a pharmacist, a fellow Genoese named Diego de Harana, who introduced him to a pretty cousin, Beatriz Enríquez. The two were smitten with each other, and before long they were living as man and wife.

Ferdinand and Isabella arrived in Córdoba in April 1486. The queen sent for Columbus on the first of May. He was confident as he awaited his audience with the king and queen. Even the location of the meeting seemed to bode well. The *alcazar,* or fortress, where the monarchs had set up court had been built by the Moors during their period of rule. During that period, Córdoba was renowned throughout all Europe for its scholars and intellectual brilliance. Indeed, many had called it the "Athens of the West," comparing it to the Greek city that had been home to the most brilliant philosophers, politicians, writers, and generals of the ancient world. Córdoba had since lost much of its luster, but Columbus felt pleased that his case would be heard in a building that had hosted so many wise men.

Columbus made his plea boldly. He had come to call on the benevolent monarchs, he said, to ask their support for a great undertaking. With their backing, and faith in God, he intended to sail west to the Orient. He had studied the work of the most learned writers on the subject; the voyage was possible. Upon arrival in the Indies, he would make contact with the Great Khan or whatever other monarchs were there and establish trade relations with those nations. Everyone knew that the Orient was filled with almost unimaginable riches; he would return to Spain with as much gold and spices as his ships could carry. He would conclude whatever political alliances the monarchs wished him to. If their majesties desired, he would even seek out Prester John, a legendary Catholic monarch whom people believed had established a Christian empire in the East. Columbus said that he would sound out Prester John about forming an alliance with Ferdinand and Isabella to reclaim the holy lands of the Levant from the Muslims. He told Ferdinand and Isabella that he expected to discover many new lands on his journey. He would claim them for Spain, and their people would be converted to Christianity. For himself, he asked only the basic requirements of his journey — ships, a crew, provisions, and expenses.

The Catholic monarchs listened impassively, asked a few questions, and then dismissed Columbus without a decision. Columbus was not discouraged by this. He knew that kings and queens preferred to deliberate over their decisions, and he was certain that he had made a strong impression, particularly on Isabella. She was his age, and he felt that she shared his intense religious beliefs. Columbus believed that his arguments regarding the lands and souls that might be converted to Christi-

Columbus petitioning King Ferdinand and Queen Isabella of Spain for their support of his journey across the Ocean Sea (the Atlantic). It took him many years to gain the royals' backing, however, mostly because they and others thought he had vastly underestimated the distance to be traveled, and they were right—he had.

anity would win her over. He felt less optimistic about Ferdinand, who had displayed distinct signs of impatience during his presentation.

Columbus's confidence waned as weeks passed without word. Finally he was informed that the monarchs themselves did not intend to make the decision. Instead, they were referring the matter to a commission headed by Hernando de Talavera, a monk who was also one of the queen's confessors. Other learned priests and scholars would make up the commission, which would meet in the city of Salamanca around Christmas of 1486. This left Columbus several months to brood over his prospects for success. The introduction of Talavera troubled him. He was held to be tolerant and wise, but in Portugal it was said that the ignorance of the priests at the Spanish court concerning geography and scientific matters was remarkable. For the last five years Isabella's other confessor, Tomás de Torquemada, had presided over the Spanish Inquisition, which was dedicated to rooting out all traces of heresy in Spain. Thousands had been tortured or executed by the Inquisition. If Talavera were ignorant, then he might interpret Columbus's assertions as heresy. If Talavera were clever, then he might prove even more dangerous; he might try to trick Columbus or to trap him into making a heretical statement. Columbus had little sense of irony, and he believed he had already endured a sort of martyrdom for the sake of his idea. The prospect of being stretched on the rack or burned at the stake did not arouse any sense of amusement in him.

At last the anticipated day arrived, and Columbus was ushered into the great room at Salamanca to make his arguments. He carefully sized up Talavera as he was presented to him. Columbus judged him to be near sixty; he was a small man, with a slight build. Time had thinned his once-full head of black hair, but his equally dark eyes still possessed a vital glow. His skin, too, was dark — although it took on a sallow tinge around his eyes — and it stretched tautly over his skull. Columbus noted that the monk's robe was trimmed with ermine and that both hands were decorated with rings, one of which was the symbol of his office as the bishop of Avila. Talavera's hand shook as Columbus knelt to kiss the ring.

Another member of the commission invited Columbus to take a seat at the long rectangular table in the center of the room, but Columbus preferred to stand. He took a position at one end of the table. Talavera sat at the opposite end. The other members of the commission took chairs on either side of Talavera, three to the right, three to the left. A number of volumes, including a Bible, and some rolled-up nautical charts tied with leather cords, rested on the middle of the table.

Talavera began the proceedings. "You are?" he said simply, with a grave nod of his head toward Columbus. His voice was much softer and lower than the mariner had expected. In another context he might even have said that it was kindly.

"I am a poor foreigner," replied Columbus, who almost never used his own name in referring to himself. He found himself admiring the sunlight that streamed onto the table through the room's high windows. Talavera's question had thrown him somewhat. Surely the monk knew who he was.

"And what do you wish?" the confessor asked. His eyes were cast down on the tabletop.

"I wish their royal majesties to fund a great trip to the East, a project I call the Enterprise of the Indies, that will bring them great glory and riches," Columbus said boldly. He went on to describe his proposal in much the same fashion as he had to Ferdinand and Isabella seven months earlier. His speech lasted for quite a long time. When he was finished, Talavera looked up at him for the first time since Columbus had begun speaking. For several moments Talavera said nothing. None of the other members of the commission seemed inclined to speak. For Columbus the silence was excruciating. The confessor finally spoke, in a low strained voice that sounded like parchment rattling.

"Surely you know that is impossible," said Talavera. "The earth is flat," the confessor said with an air of solemnity, staring directly at Columbus. Talavera's black eyes glittered. The confessor gestured over his shoulder to an unseen servant, who appeared shortly with a goblet of wine.

Columbus was stunned. As he wondered how to respond, Columbus noticed again the confessor's tremor as he lifted the goblet to his lips. Columbus's mind reeled. The Spanish were reputed to be ignorant of geography, but this was beyond belief. He decided to take a chance.

"I don't believe your grace believes that," Columbus said. He thought he saw something pass across the confessor's eyes, a flicker of light, almost like the hint of a smile on another man's face.

The bishop shakily placed the goblet on the table. "Why not?" he said. His voice was clearer, less dry.

"Because there is too much evidence that contradicts it," said Columbus. He had long since forgotten all thought of caution.

"Maybe so," Talavera said. He had built a steeple with his hands and was contemplating it. "But a northwest passage to the Orient is another matter entirely. On what authority do you base your ideas?"

"There are many," Columbus said, "but I will accomplish this because I believe in God, and He in me. He has chosen me to bring his message to the people of the East." This declaration caused some whispering between two monks to Talavera's right.

"Your faith is admirable, if unorthodox," said one of the monks with a glance at Talavera. "Yet how do you propose to carry enough provisions to see you and your men safely across the Ocean Sea, which is thousands of miles wide?"

"But it is not," replied Columbus. "Aristotle tells us that one can sail from Spain to the Indies in only a few days. Pierre D'Ailly, himself a cardinal and a prince of the church, writes that the Ocean Sea is of 'great width' and could be sailed in a short time with the aid of backing winds. Strabo, the Greek, says that only a 'want of resolution' prevented mariners of ancient times from completing the journey.

Paolo Toscanelli, a Florentine physician, mathematician, and philosopher, a student of man and the world, has written to me, enclosing a chart. He is certain that Cipangu is no more than threee thousand miles off. Even the most holy Bible contains passages which indicate that my beliefs do not contradict what God has revealed about His universe."

"That is a most interesting point, Columbus," Talavera said. "How do you respond to those who say that God has revealed all of His creation that He wants known, that man should not tempt the Almighty by seeking unknown depths of the ocean?"

"I cannot credit it. Could one have not said the same before Marco Polo made his wonderful journey? As the Lord has made use of Polo, so has He chosen me. We knew nothing of Africa until Portuguese mariners dared go there, and now its benighted hordes are being brought to Christianity."

Columbus had said his piece. After a few more perfunctory questions, the commission seemed satisfied. He was dismissed and instructed to await the commission's report to the king.

Wait Columbus did. For six long years he waited. The Enterprise of the Indies obsessed Columbus more than ever during that time. Convinced that he would soon get the go-ahead to set out for the Indies, Columbus did not take other jobs. Indeed, his reputation as an eccentric dreamer was such that few wished to hire him. Many said that he was mad. Although supporters on the commission voted to pay him a salary equivalent to that given an able-bodied seaman, he rarely received the money.

Spain was still fighting the Moors, and the war drained the treasury. At times Columbus was so poor that he could not even afford wood or fuel, and he had to burn some of his treasured nautical charts to heat the home that he and Beatriz shared. Columbus was grateful that Diego, who had remained with the Franciscans at La Rábida, did not have to see him in such dire straits. Ferdinand, his son by Beatriz, stayed with her relatives. Columbus's poverty was made even more painful by his continuing conviction that fabulous wealth was within his grasp, if only someone would to listen to him.

Desperate, Columbus wrote to King John II of Portugal in 1488, asking the king to reconsider his decision. Columbus did this even though he feared that the king might interpret his petition to Ferdinand and Isabella as evidence of disloyalty. To his surprise, King John replied in the affirmative, asking Columbus to return to Lisbon at once and promising him that he would not be arrested for the bills he had left unpaid in Lisbon. But before he could meet with King John, Bartholomew Dias, a Portuguese captain, sailed into Lisbon harbor with the news that he had rounded the southern tip of Africa and was on his way to the Orient before a mutinous crew forced his return. King John's interest in Columbus faded with the discovery of the eastern passage to the Indies.

Meanwhile, Columbus continued to wait for the verdict of the Talavera commission. His vigil wore on him. Most days he was bitter and sullen, convinced, as he wrote later, that the world's "custom of maltreating me is of very old standing." He grew thin; his once-red hair turned white. For a while he tried to start a chart-making business similar to the one he and his brother had run in Lisbon, but his heart was not in it. After a short time he abandoned the effort. He felt dispirited and weary.

Political concerns were behind the commission's delay. The commissioners did not wish to render a decision that would anger their monarchs, yet they sensed that the king and queen themselves were divided on the issue. Isabella was intrigued by the proposal and by the confident, devout Genoese mariner; Ferdinand considered the plan the height of folly. By the end of 1489, the commission could delay no more. Basing their decision on conventional wisdom, they recommended that the monarchs reject the Enterprise of the Indies. The commission said that the project "rested on weak foundations." The commission wrote that it would take three years just to reach Asia and that there was little chance the ships would be able to return. The commission also added that the Ocean Sea was much wider than Columbus and his authorities claimed and was for the most part unnavigable. Any educated person, the report concluded, would see that the project was "uncertain and impossible."

In writing to Columbus to inform him of the decision, Isabella decided to soften the blow by telling him he could petition her again in a year. The hint that the queen still possessed an interest in the

"Enterprise of the Indies" left Columbus unmoved. As he had done following his first rejection five years earlier by King John of Portugal, Columbus prepared to move on to a new country. In 1489, Columbus's brother Bartholomew had left his chart-making businesses and gone to France in order to convince the French king to underwrite Columbus's voyage. All along Bartholomew had maintained his faith in Columbus's dream of finding a western route to the Indies. Columbus made plans to be reunited with Bartholomew in France.

Before leaving Spain Columbus went to La Rábida monastery to reclaim his son Diego. His stop at La Rábida again proved fortunate. Father Juan Pérez, yet another of the scholarly Franciscans in residence there, told Columbus that he ought to submit his arguments to Isabella once again. The queen is a most wise and virtuous ruler, he told Columbus. Perhaps when the war with the Moors is over she will give you what you seek. Columbus's battered self-esteem rose in the presence of these friars, who had believed in him from the beginning. He wrote Isabella, who invited him to court and even sent him money so as to purchase a mule to travel on. She even gave him an open letter that he could use to instruct all local officials along his route to provide him with food and a place to sleep for the night.

Columbus arrived at Santa Fe, a fortified camp from which Isabella was overseeing the siege of the Moorish city of Granada, during the Christmas season of 1491. Once again he presented his arguments to the queen, this time trying, with mixed success, to keep a note of grievance out of his voice. Why had the Talavera commisson ridiculed him? he asked. Other learned men, like the Franciscans Antonio de Marchena and Juan Pérez, had not. Isabella tried in vain to assure him that his ideas had been taken seriously. Perhaps I shall go to the French, Columbus continued, seeming not to hear her. The queen was not offended. She realized that his outrage was the product of the anguish and uncertainty he had been made to endure over the years; his wounded pride she saw as further evidence of the depth of his conviction. She had seen from their first meeting that he was an unusual man; perhaps he was as special as he claimed.

The Queen asked Columbus what he wanted in return for his voyage. The weary sailor did not even stop to consider that the question might imply that Isabella was on the verge of granting what he had so long been asking for. Instead he responded without hesitation: to be granted the noble title of Admiral, to be named hereditary viceroy and governor of whatever lands he discovered, and to be granted a 10-percent share to him and his heirs of any trade with the Orient. Having endured so much for the sake of his idea, Columbus now intended to profit handsomely from its realization. All his pride, his self-confidence, his absolute conviction that he had been divinely chosen returned and were reflected in these conditions. When Isabella told him that his demands were steep, Columbus replied that the terms were not negotiable. Heeding once more the counsel of her advisers, Isabella decided that the price of the expedition had suddenly become too costly. This time, she told Columbus, her decision would not be reconsidered.

Columbus left Santa Fe, intending to return to La Rábida and from there continue on to France. But as his mule picked its leisurely way along the dusty road to La Rábida, a drama was unfolding back at Isabella's court. Luis de Santangel, King Ferdinand's treasurer, was begging Isabella to change her mind. Should Columbus's mission succeed, Santangel told his queen, it would bring Spain untold riches. The payment Columbus had asked for would amount to nothing, he argued. On the other hand, should Columbus succeed Spain would gain a vast empire and his achievements would rebound to her credit. Spain would be hailed for her wisdom and foresight. Santangel believed that the cost of funding the voyage would be small and that there was money in the treasury to do so. Even if there wasn't, Santangel went on, he himself would be willing to raise it. Columbus should be given his opportunity, the treasurer said. If, indeed, Columbus was meant by God to find the western passage, then Spain and all Christendom would reap the benefits.

Isabella was convinced. She ordered some horsemen after Columbus. They caught him at a bridge four miles away and spirited the intrepid mariner back to Santa Fe.

5

Finding a New World

RETURNING TO THE Spanish court, Columbus quickly reached an accord with Ferdinand and Isabella, who agreed to give him everything he had asked for to undertake the voyage to the Indies. A document, known as the Capitulations, was drawn up to enshrine the agreement between Columbus and the monarchs. It stipulated that Columbus had been engaged "to discover and acquire certain islands and mainlands in the Ocean Sea." He would be awarded the titles of Admiral of the Ocean Sea and viceroy and governor of all the lands he might find. As admiral, Columbus would have legal jurisdiction over all who sailed the waters he claimed for Spain. He would have the power to settle all nautical disputes that might arise, such as quarrels over fishing or trade rights. He would also have the power to try cases of piracy, mutiny, and the like. As viceroy and governor, Columbus had the power to appoint and to remove all officials in whatever lands he claimed and discovered; he would also have absolute and legal authority over Spain's new territories. In addition, the contract promised Columbus an untaxed 10 percent of all gold, silver, gems, precious metals, spices, or other goods obtained from the new lands. He would have the right to invest in one-eighth of any Spanish ship sent to trade with the Indies. These rights and privileges would pass to his sons and successors forever. Ferdinand and Isabella provided Columbus with documents stating that he had been dispatched "toward the regions of India," and a letter of introduction to the Great Khan.

Columbus spent little time celebrating his sudden good fortune. He was in a hurry to begin the long-awaited voyage. Leaving Diego and Ferdinand with Beatriz in Seville, Columbus made his way to Palos, from where the expedition was to depart. This time Columbus made the trip on horseback. The miles fairly flew by, and it seemed to Columbus that the greatest part of his struggle was over. He had no doubt that he would reach the Indies. All he had lacked were the means to carry out his ideas. That he would succeed now was beyond question. The years of poverty and obscurity, of derision and scorn, were behind him; of this Columbus was certain. Ahead lay glory and riches, fame and new lands.

Columbus found it appropriate that Palos, the dusty village that had been his first stop as a disappointed refugee from the court of Portugal's King

John, should now see him off on what promised to be the greatest voyage of exploration the world had known. The city, whose sleepy docks had so disappointed Columbus upon his arrival from cosmopolitan Lisbon, was actually a convenient point of departure.

Columbus stopped once more at La Rábida, the monastery on the bluffs four miles outside of Palos. The Franciscan monks there who had given Columbus refuge upon his arrival from Portugal were eager to celebrate his turn in providence. A Mass was said in the monastery's chapel; with bowed head Columbus thanked God for his good fortune. On May 23, 1492, Columbus attended another Mass, this time at the Church of St. George in Palos itself. The town's citizens turned out to catch a glimpse of the intrepid mariner who was about to brave the Ocean Sea and sail to Asia. Again, Columbus thanked the Lord for singling him out as His representative to bring His gospel to the East. He felt no need to ask that his voyage be a success; he had known for years that it would be. At the Mass's conclusion Father Juan Pérez read the proclamation from Queen Isabella requiring the city of Palos to supply Columbus with two ships and their crews within ten days' time.

It took closer to three months to outfit the expedition. The two ships that the city of Palos provided were named the *Niña* and the *Pinta*. Both were caravels, comparatively small, fast vessels with high poop decks and short masts. The ships were designed to carry three lateen, or triangular, sails, although Columbus had both rigged with square sails. The *Niña* was aboutseventy 70 feet long, with a cargo capacity of sixty tons; the *Pinta* was slightly larger. As Columbus supervised the preparation of the ships, he imagined that day when the holds of both would be filled with precious metals and costly spices from the Indies. Two brothers commanded the ships. Martin Alonso Pinzón captained the *Pinta*; Vicente Yáñez Pinzón was in charge of the *Niña*.

Columbus's flagship, the *Santa María,* was a slightly larger vessel. It was of the type the Portuguese called a *nao*, an all-purpose term designating a large ship. The *Santa María* had a capacity of 100 tons and carried three huge square sails. Columbus chartered his flagship from a local shipbuilder, Juan de la Cosa, who agreed to ship out as a member of the Expedition of the Indies.

Initially his fleet did not please Columbus. None of the ships was new, and they seemed shabby and cumbersome in comparison with the elegant Portuguese vessels he was used to. Although not a man of discretion by temperament, Columbus kept his mouth shut. He did not want to jeopardize his voyage on the eve of its departure.

Columbus's crew turned out to be equally motley. The queen had promised four months' advance pay — the equivalent of $28 in gold — to any sailor who signed up for the voyage. However, this did not appear to be enough to attract the sailors of the Niebla, the region where Palos was located. The sailors of the day were a notoriously superstitious lot. Few wished to venture into the unknown. Some still believed the earth to be flat, while others had heard that gruesome sea monsters prowled the depths of the Ocean Sea west of the Azores. Still, the chance for wealth and adventure convinced at least some to sign up for the voyage; others were bullied and cajoled by the authorities of Palos, who were obligated to provide a crew. Finally, however, with the ships still short several hands, the jails were emptied; a handful of criminals were pardoned in exchange for shipping out with Columbus. Columbus knew he would have a hard time instilling discipline in these men. Though the Pinzóns and de la Cosa seemed very competent, the others were like most sailors, Columbus thought — selfish and shortsighted. It would be a miracle if the sailors didn't panic at the first sight of misfortune.

The three ships hoisted their anchors in the early morning of August 3, hours before dawn. Columbus led the men aboard the *Santa María* in silent prayer and gave the order to cast off.

Columbus smiled as his ship gained the open sea. It had been nine years since he had commanded an oceangoing vessel. He had worried that the sea might have lost its charm for him, but his fears were unfounded. A magnificent sun rose and cast its benevolent rays upon a placid ocean. Above the towering masts gulls wheeled and called to one another in the blue sky. The men of the *Santa María* bantered among themselves with all the good nature of sailors returned to the sea. A steady breeze sped the *Niña, Pinta,* and the *Santa María* on their way. Before noon the last trace of land had vanished behind them.

The fleet headed south, to the Canary Islands, where they took on additional provisions and made minor repairs. The ships left the Canary Islands on September 6, and turned west. Columbus believed he would find strong backing winds and good weather at these southern latitudes. He was right. Glorious days followed. Favorable winds and calm seas prevailed. Each morning's sunrise was a thing of beauty. The fleet made remarkable time, and the mystical Columbus saw in the clear skies an omen of success.

All went well with the voyage until mid-September. Columbus had known from the outset that the optimism of his crew was superficial. In truth, it barely disguised their skepticism and mistrust. The crew began to grumble when the legendary island of Antilia did not appear where the charts said it should be. This fact did not bother Columbus much, since he was in a hurry to reach the Indies, but it greatly disturbed the crew. The next week poor winds slowed the fleet's progress. The crew began to wonder aloud how they would ever make it back to Spain given the prevalence of east winds.

As September gave way to October, the days grew filled with wild talk among the crew about sea monsters and a mad captain. The crew's unrest was now general. Sensing that the men were on the verge of mutiny, Columbus addressed them early on the morning of October 6. He reminded them of their duty, appealed to their desire for riches and

The first journey to the New World was fraught with difficulty. Columbus's crew threatened mutiny when the caravels failed to reach land in the time Columbus said they would. Contrary to popular belief, they did not fear "falling off the edge of the world." Rather, the strong winds that always blew from the east made them wonder whether they would be able to make the return voyage to Spain.

fame, and asked them to put their trust in God and in him. Had one sailor defied Columbus on that day, the other sailors most likely would have joined in. Columbus's certainty convinced them, however, as it had convinced Ferdinand and Isabella. The surly crew returned to its duties.

A few days later, the Pinzóns, the captains of the *Niña* and the *Pinta*, brought their ships in close to the *Santa María* to confer with the captain-general. They were worried that the ships had traveled too far. They thought Columbus had been mistaken, and that it would be prudent to turn back. But Columbus would not be swayed. He replied in a voice that was both commanding and pleading that he had sailed to find the Indies and that, with the Lord's help, he was going to find them. It was agreed that if land was not sighted in three days, the ships would reverse course. "Sail on, then, sail on!" Martin Alonso Pinzón yelled, but to Columbus his words sounded hollow and forced. The three small ships stormed westward, the fearful eyes of their crews fixed on the horizon in the hope they might spot land.

Spirits lightened around noon on October 11, as the crew began to see tree branches with green leaves on them adrift in the ocean, a clear sign that land must be near. The crew members congratulated each other on their bravery. They talked about the noble titles they would soon sport, the fine clothes they would wear, the magnificent stallions they would ride, and the gold and silver that would fill the pockets of each and every one of them. But their captain seemed unmoved. Indeed, he appeared grimmer and more determined than ever, and he spoke not a word.

But that night, at about ten o'clock, Columbus cried out that he saw a light on the horizon, "like a little wax candle rising and falling," as he later described it. A few other seamen saw it, too. But most of the sailors saw nothing, and doubts about the captain-general's sanity rose anew. The ships sped onward, everyone tense and watchful. Finally, at 2 o'clock in the morning, Rodrigo de Triana, high in the rigging of the *Pinta*, screamed, "Land! Land!" Martin Alonso Pinzón raced to the railing and confirmed his watchman's sighting. As arranged previously, he fired a cannon to let Columbus know that they had reached the Indies. Columbus, however, had already seen land for himself and had dropped to his knees on the deck to give thanks to the Lord. His prayer was drowned out by the wild shouts and cheering of his men.

At daybreak Columbus went ashore, accompanied by the two Pinzóns and some of the crew. After planting the royal flags of Castile and Aragon, Columbus knelt on the coral beach and wept "tears of joy for the immeasurable mercy of having reached it," as he wrote later. He gave his discovery the name *San Salvador*, which in English means Holy Savior.

6

An Incomparable Land

AS COLUMBUS ROSE from kneeling in prayer to God, he was aware that he and his men were not alone. He knew that dark eyes were watching him from the dense forest of tropical trees. He had seen human figures on the beach when the small boat carrying him and the others in the landing party set out from the bay where the *Niña, Pinta,* and the *Santa María* were anchored. Columbus had assumed that these were emissaries of the Great Khan or the ruler of Japan and that they had come to greet him. To his surprise, however, they had fled at the approach of his boat. The beach was empty.

This last was just one more factor in the confusion that Columbus was feeling. He had expected that upon reaching the Indies he would find busy harbors filled with ships and merchants. But his fleet had sailed halfway around San Salvador, and nothing of the sort existed. There were plenty of pristine harbors, beautiful sandy beaches, exotic plants, and brightly colored birds, but no signs of a great civilization or the Great Khan. Columbus concluded that he had landed on a hitherto unknown island in the Indies. He hoped that he was not too far from China or Cipangu. By all his calculations, he should have been right on target.

What Columbus did not realize was that he had not reached Asia at all. Talavera and the other monks and geographers had been correct — Asia was over 10,000 miles away and could not be reached by sailing due west from the Canaries. But Columbus had been right, too — there were new lands to be discovered to the west, although they were not part of the Indies, as he believed. Neither Columbus nor the learned scholars of the day realized that two continents — North America and South America — lay to the west between Europe and Asia. It would take another thirty years for a Portuguese explorer, Ferdinand Magellan, to discover the westward passage to the Indies. Columbus had discovered a small island in what is known today as the Caribbean Sea. The island that Columbus chose to call San Salvador was known to its inhabitants as Guanahani. Today it is believed that Columbus landed on Watling Island in the Bahamas.

After a short time, the island's native inhabitants, overcome by curiosity, made their way out of the forest and onto the beach to greet the newcomers. Their physical appearance impressed Columbus, who noted in a letter he wrote later to Ferdinand and Isabella that they were "well-built people of handsome stature." He was taken by their "flowing" black hair and apparent gentleness, but most of all by their nakedness. It also did not escape his notice that that many of the natives wore gold pendants in their noses and on their ears.

The two groups eyed each other on the beach, both careful not to say or do anything that would frighten the other. Columbus beckoned his interpreter forward, but the man's attempts at conversation drew only uncomprehending stares from the Indians, who, when they spoke, did so in a tongue unknown to the interpreters. Columbus had taken along an interpreter fluent in Arabic, because it had been assumed that this was the language the Great Khan and his people would speak.

Columbus was surprised but not fazed by what he beheld. This new land's inhabitants were bronze skinned rather than yellow, as he had expected. They did not speak Arabic. And they wore no clothing at all — a far cry from the brilliant-colored robes trimmed with precious stones he had imagined. Still, Columbus remained ever confident. He was so certain that he had reached the Indies that he dubbed the people "Indios," which in Spanish means "inhabitants of the Indies." This term has come down to us as the word *Indians*.

Although the Arabic interpreter proved to be useless, the two groups were able to communicate through sign language and gesture. The Spaniards let the Indians know that they were interested in the gold from which the Indian pendants and earrings had been fashioned. The Indians seemed delighted with the trinkets — glass beads, red caps, small brass bells — that the Spaniards had brought as trade offerings. They indicated to the Spaniards that there was gold to be found on nearby islands.

Columbus marveled at the innocence of the Indians. "They are wonderfully timorous," he wrote Ferdinand and Isabella, "timid beyond cure . . . They are so artless and so free with all they possess, that no one would believe it without having seen it. Of anything they have, if you ask them for it, they never say no; rather they invite the person to share it, and show as much love as if they were giving their hearts; and whether the thing be of value or of small price, at once they are content with whatever little thing of whatever kind may be given to them."

Though Columbus had not found the great cities of the East, he was pleased at having found evidence of gold. More important, the people he had found were docile and trusting — they had no iron or steel weapons, and even if they did, thought Columbus, they wouldn't by nature be able to use them. This led him to believe that the Indians would give their gold to the Spanish. In the log in which he recorded the impressions intended for his eyes only, Columbus wrote, "[They were] very cowardly . . . fit to be ordered about and made to work, to sow and do [whatever] else that may be needed." Because the Indians were not Christians, Columbus believed that they could be enslaved and converted without the Spanish feeling any guilt. "How easy it would be," Columbus wrote, "to convert these people — and to make them work for us."

After a few days of exploring on the island, Columbus was convinced that the San Salvador Indians were telling the truth in saying that gold was to be found only on nearby islands. Kidnapping six Indians to serve as guides, Columbus and his men pushed on. Columbus believed that each new stop would reveal one of the fabled cities of Cipangu or China, but he found only a succession of small islands similar to San Salvador. Columbus saw many new things at which he marveled — fields of Indian corn, yams, woven cotton hammocks, and trees and animals not known to the Spaniards — but no cities, no Great Khan, and no gold.

Columbus grew frustrated. New islands were fine, but the monarchs would want some material benefit to show for their investment. Although Columbus felt vindicated by having demonstrated, at least to his own satisfaction, that he had been right about sailing west to reach the Indies, he wanted more than moral satisfaction. He wanted wealth. Listening to the natives talk among themselves, he heard repeated mention of a place called Colba, which the Indians seemed to indicate was a large island. "Bring me there," Columbus ordered his guides, having already convinced himself that Colba must be either Japan or part of China.

Colba turned out to be the island known today as Cuba. Columbus admired its verdant forests, abundant wildlife, and beautiful natural harbors. But it was not China or Japan. There were no sophisticated Orientals there. Rather, the inhabitants turned out to be more naked Indians. However, they did tell Columbus that gold could be found at a large city in the interior known as Cubanacan. To Columbus, the name sounded like the Great Khan. He dispatched a search party consisting of the interpreter and another sailor, who carried with them the letter of introduction from Ferdinand and Isabella to the Great Khan. Alas, the great city turned out to be a small village of palm-thatched huts. Still, the Spaniards were treated graciously by the villagers, for the Indians believed the Spaniards were gods who had descended from the sky. Among the many curiosities seen by the visitors was the rolling of an herb into long cylindrical shapes that were then smoked. The herb the Indians used is known today as tobacco.

Columbus was not amused by the tales with which his search party returned. He dutifully recorded his impressions of the island, which he named Juana, in his log, but his appreciation for nature's charms was waning. To Columbus, that land that was most beautiful was land that yielded up gold or silver. Finally, with a feeling of resignation, he began to make a collection of new species of fauna that the expedition had uncovered. He hoped that these would convince Isabella that the trip had at least been of scientific interest.

Columbus was not the only person who was disappointed. His crew shared his feelings. At first the men had been so excited at finding land that they had forgotten the disgruntlement they had felt on board. But then they remembered that they had been promised great riches and fame. After more than a month of sailing from island to island, however, they had begun to lose patience. So far they had only uncovered a few small nuggets of gold. Thus, when Martin Alonso Pinzón, the captain of the *Pinta*, understood an Indian to say that there was an island nearby where Indian men gathered gold at night off of the beaches, he and his crew sailed off in search of it without saying a word to Columbus. Columbus did not send anyone after Pinzón, having no time to waste on this act of insubordination. If Pinzón was foolish enough to sail alone in uncharted waters, with no fellow ships to aid him in case of trouble, then so be it.

Privately, Columbus was approaching the point of despair. He was beginning to wonder if the Lord was playing him for a fool. Nevertheless he pressed onward along the northern coast of the island of Juana. At the direction of his Indian guides, he crossed an expanse of open sea and after a short time sighted a great island, which impressed him with its grandeur and beauty and its resemblance to the land of Spain. He named it *La Isla Española,* the Spanish Isle. It was since come to be known as Hispaniola. This is how he described the island in a letter to King Ferdinand and Queen Isabella:

"In it there are many harbors on the coast of the sea, incomparable to others which I know in Christendom, and numerous rivers, good and large, which is marvelous. Its lands are lofty and in it there are many sierras and very high mountains, to which the island Tenerife [one of the Canary Islands] is not comparable. All are most beautiful, of a thousand shapes, and all accessible and filled with trees of a thousand kinds and tall, and they seem to touch the sky; and I am told that they never lose their foliage, which I can believe, for I saw them as green and beautiful as they are in Spain in May, and some of them were flowering, some with fruit, and some in other condition, according to their quality. And there were singing the nightingale and other little birds of a thousand kinds in the month of November, there where I went. There are palm trees of six or eight kinds, which are a wonder to behold on account of their beautiful variety, and so are the other trees and fruits and herbs; therein are marvelous pine groves, and extensive champagne country; and there is honey, and there are many kinds of birds and a great variety of fruits. Upcountry there are many mines of metals, and the population is innumerable. Hispaniola is marvelous, the sierras and the mountains and the plains and the champagnes and the lands are so beautiful and so fat for planting and sowing, and for livestock of every sort, and for building towns and cities. The harbors of the sea here are such as you could not believe in without seeing them, and so the rivers, many and great, and good streams, the most of which bear gold. And the trees and fruits and plants have great differences from those of La Juana; in this there are many spices and great mines of gold and of other metals."

This last point regarding its gold mines was Hispaniola's most important selling point, in Columbus's view. Indeed, it made Columbus receptive to the island's other blessings. The Indians there were equally gentle and friendly. On December 16, 1492, 500 natives came to the beach near where the two Spanish ships lay anchored. They were led by their chieftain, who had decorated himself in gold jewelry such as the Great Khan himself would have been proud to own. Columbus invited the tribal leader to dine aboard the *Santa María* and was relieved to learn that Hispaniola was rich in gold and precious jewels. A week later, at another harbor farther along Hispaniola's coast, 1,500 natives paddled canoes or swam out to greet the Spanish vessels, which they believed were great white-winged birds descended from the heavens. Virtually all of them, Columbus noticed, wore gold. That night a messenger from a chieftain who lived farther down the coast arrived, bearing a magnificent gold belt buckle as a propitiatory gift. Columbus had never seen such a beautiful gold belt. He remained awake that night until dawn, fasting and praying, in penance for doubting the Lord's benevolence.

Early on the morning of December 24, Christmas Eve, the *Santa María* and the *Niña* set sail for the land of Guacanagarí, the Indian chieftain who had sent Columbus the gold belt buckle. The weather was not favorable, and the two ships fought the winds all day. By eleven o'clock that night they had sailed only a few miles. There was no wind at all. The men on board had not gotten much sleep for

On Christmas Day 1492 the Santa Maria *was* wrecked on a reef on the coast of Hispaniola, one of several islands Columbus explored in the Indies. The help he received from friendly Indians during the calamity led him to select the island as the site of a Spanish settlement.

the past couple of days; Columbus himself had not slept for forty-eight hours. The night was calm and peaceful. Columbus felt that the weather was befitting Christmas Eve. He dismissed the crew, except for the helmsman, and then retired to catch some sleep. The helmsman was exhausted and felt resentful at having to remain on duty while the others slept. He made a ship's boy take the wheel and went to bed.

Columbus was awakened shortly after midnight on Christmas Day by the alarmed cry of the ship's boy. He discovered after arriving on deck that the *Santa María* had drifted onto a coral reef and settled there. The *Santa María's* hull had been ripped open and the ship was filling with water. Columbus and his crew were forced to spend Christmas Day transferring personnel and cargo to the *Niña*. They were aided by the Indians, who rowed out to help them. Columbus was amazed that the Indians did not attempt to profit by the expedition's predicament.

The misfortune brought the expedition to the Indies to an end. With Martin Alonso Pinzón gone in search of gold on the other ship, only one ship remained. Columbus could not afford to explore the island further and take the risk of damaging the last ship. No rescue missions would be sent from Spain should that happen, he was sure. No one in Europe even knew where he was. He could imagine the wags at Ferdinand and Isabella's court clucking their tongues, shaking their heads, and laughing about that crazy Genoese who had sailed west and never been heard from again. It was more important that he return to Spain with the news of his success. Although Columbus dreaded an ocean voyage without a second ship to accompany him, it was the only course available to him.

Given his religious temperament, Columbus saw the divine hand of God at work in all that had happened to him. He interpreted the shipwreck as a heavenly message. As the island needed to be secured for Spain, the Lord meant for Columbus to establish a colony near the spot where the *Santa María* had run aground. Columbus decided that he would call it Navidad, the Spanish word for Christmas.

The Admiral had no trouble securing volunteers to stay behind. His crewmen figured life on Hispaniola would be easy. There was gold, the Indians would do all the work for them, the weather seemed nice, and they could get a head start on claiming the lands that would be their estates in the new Spanish colony. Few gave any thought to practical questions such as how they would grow food or what they would do when their shoes wore out. The *Santa María* was stripped of its wood, which was used to build the first European fort in the New World. On December 31, 1492, the Indians and the Spaniards rang in the New Year together. On January 3, the crew of the *Niña* bid farewell to the thirty-nine comrades who were remaining behind, and the small, square-rigged caravel started out on the return journey to Spain.

Columbus was more apprehensive about the return voyage than he had been about the voyage going out. Nothing would be worse, he thought, than for a storm or some other catastrophe to send his ship to the ocean bottom with the news of his discoveries still unknown to the rest of the world. Columbus disliked sailing alone, and he was uncertain about his return route. In fact, despite his words to the crew in quieting the mutiny that had been brewing on the voyage to the New World, he had no definite return route in mind. He knew only that the winds at the latitudes he had come on would be unfavorable, and planned to sail home in more northerly waters. Beyond that, he would trust to his instinct. Luckily, this had not failed him yet.

Columbus hoped to reach Spain in a hurry. He did not know what Martin Pinzón on the *Pinta* had been up to since parting company with the other ships, and he did not wish Pinzón to beat him back to Spain and steal his thunder. Those fears disappeared when the *Niña* encountered the *Pinta* two days out of Hispaniola. Pinzón was all apologies at having gone off in search of gold. Columbus accepted the apologies. His happiness at having another ship for the voyage outweighed his anger at Pinzón's disobedience.

The two ships had difficulty finding favorable winds, and they made fitful progress. In mid-February, while passing north of the Azores, they sailed into the teeth of a fierce gale. Powerful winds whipped up the ocean into a violent frenzy. Monstrous waves lashed the ships' hulls and crashed

81

across the decks. Having depleted the stores of provisions in their holds, the ships were much lighter now. They were pitched and tossed helplessly on the turbulent sea. The *Niña* and *Pinta* were soon separated.

As the tempest raged with no sign of letting up, the sailors aboard the *Niña* drew lots to determine who would make a pilgrimage to a shrine of the Blessed Virgin should they be spared from the storm. The ocean seemed not to hear. The wind howled louder, the day turned black as night, and the waves swelled higher. In desperation, the entire crew, including Columbus, vowed that they would all make a pilgrimage, clad only in their shirts as a sign of penitence, should they be saved from death. Convinced that he would never see land again, Columbus hurriedly prepared a digest of his journal, containing the most important facts about his discoveries. He sealed it in a small wine cask and tossed it overboard, hoping that it would be recovered and be passed on to Ferdinand and Isabella.

The next morning a sailor spotted land dead ahead. It was one of the Azores, but the wind was now so fierce that it took the skilled Columbus three days to pilot the *Niña* to a safe landing. As if preordained, the *Niña* had anchored near a small fishing village called Our Lady of the Angels, which featured a shrine to the Blessed Virgin. The overjoyed sailors, dressed only in their shirts, poured into the chapel to give thanks for being saved from the storm.

Unfortunately, the Spaniards were not safe yet. The Azores were Portuguese territory. Hearing of the sudden influx of partly undressed and bedraggled Spanish sailors, the governor of the island concluded that the newcomers had been trading ilegally in Portugal's West African colonies. Accompanied by his townsmen, the governor stormed into the chapel where the Spaniards were praying and placed them under arrest. He then rowed out to the *Niña*, intending to arrest Columbus and the three sailors who were watching over the ship.

Columbus looked at the governor in disbelief. He could not believe his ears and quickly became indignant. Did this half-crazed provincial politician think that he could stop Columbus, the Admiral of the Ocean Sea, on the brink of completing his mission? Columbus bellowed for the governor to get off his ship, and told him that he expected the immediate release of his men from jail, or he would ransack the town. It was a threat that Columbus could not have carried out. He had only three men and the six Indian guides. Fortunately, the weather intervened before he could act. The storm blew up again. The winds blew so hard that the *Niña* snapped its cables and was driven far out to sea.

Several days passed before Columbus and what remained of his crew could maneuver back to the shipping village, and to Our Lady of the Angels. By the time they arrived the governor had decided that his captives were telling him the truth and that they had not been involved in illegal trade with

Africa. All the sailors of the *Niña* were released, and the town offered to stock the ship with provisions.

The *Niña* resumed its homeward voyage. On the night of March 2, 1493, as the *Niña* neared the coast of Portugal, it sailed right into a cyclone. Winds that "seemed to raise the caravel into the air" tore the *Niña*'s sails to shreds and toppled its masts. The battered ship pressed on until it reached the entrance of the Tagus River.

Columbus now faced yet another dilemma. The Portuguese capital of Lisbon lay eight miles up the Tagus. The most prudent course would have been to take shelter from the storm in the river channel, and then to proceed to Lisbon to ask King John II's permission to put in for repairs. Yet who could tell how the king would greet his former subject? He would not be happy to learn that Columbus had succeeded in a mission for his archrivals, Ferdinand and Isabella of Spain. King John might throw the entire crew in jail. Still, it might be possible to get a message from Lisbon to the Spanish court. Columbus hoped to get news of his discoveries to Ferdinand and Isabella before Martin Pinzón did. It was this last consideration that convinced Columbus that he should ask the Portuguese king for permission to repair his ship.

The *Niña* headed up the Tagus and anchored at Lisbon. Columbus sent a messenger ashore to ask the Portuguese king's permission to make repairs. King John was in the midst of a retreat at a monastery, so his response was several days in coming. As it turned out, the king was very glad to hear from his old friend Columbus. His messenger told the wary Genoese that the King had instructed the merchants of Lisbon to provide him with everything he might need, free of charge, and that the king would also consider it an honor for Columbus to visit him. Although anxious to reach Spain, Columbus could not refuse the invitation. He wanted to see the expression on the king's face when he told him of his discoveries.

Taking a few of his sailors and the Indians with him, the admiral journeyed to the monastery where the king was staying. Columbus found the king's reaction to be worth the inconvenience of the trip. The monarch greeted Columbus warmly and listened impassively while the admiral boasted of his finds. His advisers, though, were not so pleased, and they urged the king to have the impertinent traitor assassinated. The king refused, mostly because he was sure that Columbus was lying. Then Columbus asked the Indians to make a chart of their home islands, using some beans from their native lands. This demonstration convinced the king, who began sobbing and beating his breast with his hand. "Why did I let slip such a wonderful chance?" the remorseful king whimpered.

King John did indeed allow Columbus to dispatch a message to the Spanish court — the long letter he had written about what he had seen and discovered in the Indies. At the same time, unbeknownst to Columbus, the *Pinta* had already landed off the Spanish coast, and Martin Pinzón had sent a messenger to Ferdinand and Isabella asking their permission to come to court and to tell them of the trip to the Indies. From Barcelona, in northeast Spain, the Catholic monarchs gave Pinzón a quick response: Stay where you are, they replied, we are waiting to hear directly from Columbus.

On March 13 the *Niña* left Portugal on the last leg of its journey. The following morning it passed by the beach, near Palos, where Columbus had washed up after the battle with the French years before. How modest his dreams had seemed then, Columbus thought; how paltry in comparison with what he had achieved! Two days later the *Niña* and its plucky captain and crew anchored at Palos, their incredible journey at an end. On that day Columbus made the final journal entry for the voyage. Columbus's words reflected the personal faith that had driven and sustained him, the certainty that he had been divinely ordained to perform unprecedented feats. He wrote: "Of this voyage I observe that the will of God hath miraculously been set forth, on this voyage and for myself, who for so great a time was in the court of Your Highnesses, with the opposition and against the opinion of so many personages of your household, who were all against me, alleging this undertaking to be folly, which I hope in Our Lord will be to the greater glory of Christianity."

Once ashore, Columbus hurried to a nearby shrine to pay his respects to the Blessed Virgin. He then proceeded to the monastery at La Rábida, where he had a joyful reunion with the monks there. After a month, he received the message he had been waiting for; his letter had reached Ferdinand and Isabella. Their reply was addressed to "Don Cristóbal Colón, their admiral of the Ocean Sea, Viceroy and Governor of the islands that he hath discovered in the Indies." Columbus needed to read no further; the monarchs' greeting meant that, in reward for his service to Spain, he had been awarded all the titles he had sought.

Columbus's journey to the royal court at Barcelona was a triumphal procession. It seemed to him as if all of Spain had turned out to see the intrepid mariner who had sailed to Asia. Black-robed priests, arrogant nobles, curious merchants, stiff-backed soldiers, wealthy landowners, tired peasants straight from the field and grateful for the afternoon's holiday — all lined the routes of the parade. All crowded against one another and craned their necks to catch a glimpse of Columbus, the white-haired admiral astride his black stallion, the Genoan who had become Spain's greatest hero.

7

Colonizing the New World

COLUMBUS WAS THE man of the hour. King
Ferdinand and Queen Isabella were fascinated with his story. They closely examined the
gold samples he'd brought back and questioned the
Indians at great length. They studied the spices and
plants that Columbus had collected. Columbus was
toasted at lavish state dinners, and a special Mass of
thanksgiving for the success of his mission was
said. His fame spread throughout Spain and beyond, and scientists and scholars discussed his
travels and discoveries. Copies of his letter were
printed and published in Spain and Italy, where
they were particularly popular.

Columbus spent little time reveling in his leisure.
After enjoying a brief but joyous reunion with
Beatriz and his children, he began to make plans
almost immediately for a return voyage to the lands
that he had discovered. Ferdinand and Isabella

were anxious to provide anything that might be needed to carry out Columbus's ambitious plan for establishing a trading colony on Hispaniola. The monarchs declared that the second voyage was to have three objectives: the conversion of the natives to Christianity, the establishment of a trading colony, and the exploration of Cuba to determine whether it was part of China.

Although Columbus had originally believed that Cuba was an island, his certainty that he must have reached the Indies caused him to rethink his ideas. He now felt that Cuba was the southern part of China and hoped that further exploration of the region would reveal the legendary cities of the Great Khan. The second voyage, he was sure, would be even more successful than the first. His conviction that he had been favored by heaven grew stronger, and the mystical and religious aspects of his character grew even more pronounced. He adopted a curious symbol, a mixture of Greek and Roman letters, as his signature. The letters were meant to signify "Servant am I of the most high Jesus Christ." By using them he wished to emphasize his role as the missionary who had brought Christianity to the Indies.

Preparations for Columbus's second journey to the Indies began in June 1493. Whereas the first trip had been a voyage of discovery, this second was to be primarily a colonizing expedition. The town of Palos, which had outfitted the first expedition, was not up to the task of outfitting the huge fleet that was needed. Instead a fleet was assembled at Cadiz,

Columbus at court in Barcelona in 1493 upon his triumphant
return from the New World. Among the items he displayed for
Ferdinand and Isabella were Indians, parrots, plants, dolls,
weapons, clothing, household utensils, musical instruments,
and vegetables such as corn and potatoes, which were not
known in Spain.

a beautiful port city of white houses on the southern coast of Spain. Columbus had no trouble rounding up men and ships for this journey. Indeed, it seemed as if everyone was eager to help establish Spain's colony on Hispaniola. There would be room for 1,200 men aboard the seventeen vessels Columbus proposed to take with him this time, and the Admiral had many more volunteers to choose from than there were positions available. Among the 1,200 men finally chosen to sail were 6 missionaries, who were to convert the Indians; Columbus's youngest brother, Diego; and a young Spaniard named Juan Ponce de León, who would gain fame some years later for his own voyages of exploration. There were also 300 *hidalgos*, members of the Spanish nobility, who were eager to claim great estates for themselves on Hispaniola.

In addition to the men, the ships carried the materials that the Spaniards thought would be necessary to establish a successful trading colony. Muskets and ammunition, hundreds of casks of wine, horses, cows, mules, a score of fierce mastiff dogs, dozens of tins of hardtack, seeds for planting wheat and grains, farm implements, carpentry tools, and barrels of fresh water filled the holds of the ships that comprised the Spanish fleet.

All was ready by September 25. That morning, the "united and handsome" fleet, in Columbus's words, left Cadiz. Gorgeous weather accompanied the Spanish vessels on their way west, just as it had on Columbus's first voyage. Favorable winds prevailed, and the fleet made fine time.

Columbus followed a course similar to that of the first voyage. The only difference was that he made allowances so that the fleet would sail toward a number of islands to the west of Hispaniola. The Indians claimed that one of these was occupied only by women, and that the others were home to fearsome cannibals known as the "Caribs." Little thought was given to the sailors from the first voyage who had stayed behind at Navidad. Columbus was in no rush to check on their progress. He took it for granted that the Spaniards would be able to survive and prosper among the pagan and inferior Indians.

The expedition fleet reached land early on the morning of November 5, 1493. It was a Sunday, and so Columbus named the great new island Dominica; *Domingo* is the Spanish word for Sunday. Sailing on instinct, Columbus continued with his fleet through a treacherous, shallow passage among coral reefs and into the island group known today as the Lesser Antilles. Columbus named these after various shrines to the Virgin Mary. A landing party was sent to explore a large island that Columbus called Guadeloupe. However, the men became lost in the dense tropical rain forest and had to be rescued by a search party. When the members of the landing party returned to the ships they told harrowing tales of abandoned huts in which they found human bones picked clean, partly consumed human flesh, and young boys being raised to serve as future meals. The fleet hurriedly moved on.

The crew members found it hard to believe that the islands were inhabited by the bloodthirsty Caribs, for the natural beauty of the islands through which they were sailing was awe inspiring. Tall volcanic mountains towered thousands of feet above the clear Caribbean. Spectacular waterfalls cascaded from mountainous crevices. But it soon became clear that the Indian inhabitants of these islands were indeed much less friendly than their counterparts on the island of Hispaniola. On November 14, Columbus sent a small boat manned by twenty-five Spaniards to explore a cove off the island known today as St. Croix. They were set upon by six Caribs in a canoe, and a skirmish ensued. One Spaniard was killed by an arrow, and several Caribs met their death. The rest of the Caribs were taken captive. The fight convinced the Spanish that the stories they had been told about the Caribs' ferocity had not been exaggerated. From that point on, they tried to steer clear of the cannibals.

For the next week, Columbus and his fleet made their way westward, in the process discovering the lands known today as Puerto Rico and the Virgin Islands. At last, on November 24, they landed on Hispaniola. It took them the next couple of days to sail along the island's north shore to the Spanish settlement, Navidad. The fleet arrived at nightfall. Remembering that the *Santa María* had foundered on a coral reef, Columbus chose not to risk tearing the bottom out of any of his boats by attempting a nighttime landing. Instead he announced his arrival by lighting some flares and firing his cannons.

There was no response from the Spanish fort. At daybreak, a few Indians sailed out to the Spanish ships in canoes and assured Columbus that the Spanish colony ashore was faring just fine. A few Spaniards had taken ill, they said.

Columbus soon discovered that the Indians had lied about conditions at the Spanish settlement. The actual situation was more serious. Unwilling to do any work themselves — to clear the land, to plant crops, or to mine for gold, for example — the Spaniards at Navidad had lost little time in demanding that the Indians give them what they wanted. They demanded gold, food, and women. They formed raiding parties and roamed the island, terrorizing villages, stealing gold and food and kidnapping men and women to work as slaves. Not surprisingly, the Indians soon tired of such treatment and retaliated. First they ambushed a Spanish raiding party and succeeded in killing all its members. The few remaining Spaniards at Navidad were no match for the mass of Indians who attacked them and were wiped out completely.

The news of the fate of the colonists at Navidad spread like wildfire among the men of the new expedition. They demanded immediate retaliation. It took all of Columbus's skills of persuasion to convince them that such action would be folly. The men reluctantly accepted their leader's reasoning, but they were not happy with him. They tauntingly reminded Columbus of his assertions that the Indians were timid, cowardly, and docile. The massacre also affected Columbus's attempts to found a new

Spanish colony. He had no choice but to conclude that Navidad was an unsuitable site for the Spanish trading post. Instead he led his fleet eastward, to another part of the island. He named the new post Isabela, in honor of the queen who had believed in his vision.

Columbus wanted to create a traditional Spanish city in the wilderness of Hispaniola. He had drawn up detailed plans laying out blocks and streets, a church, a governor's palace fronting a classic Spanish plaza, and more. Work details were formed, and Columbus set the would-be colonists to work chopping down trees, quarrying stone, digging canals, and building huts to serve as temporary housing. Few of the 1,200 men who had accompanied Columbus on the voyage were happy about this situation. They had been told that the living was easy on Hispaniola, yet this Genoan had them working like dray horses. Why should they sweat when there were all these Indians who could do the work for them? The Spanish noblemen especially were indignant. They considered themselves gentlemen and felt manual labor to be beneath them. When Columbus proved unyielding and insisted that they do their share, opposition to his leadership grew. Many proud and patriotic Spaniards began to grumble about having to take orders from a Genoan.

The situation was worsened by the site Columbus had chosen for the establishment of Isabela. It was far from any source of fresh water and was infested with mosquitos. The Spaniards began to contract malaria in large numbers. Unwilling to plant their own fields or to fish, the colonists had to rely on what the Indians would give them for food. But the native Indian diet did not agree with the Europeans, and hundreds more fell sick. All of this served only to increase discontent with Columbus's governmental policies. The Spaniards began to send raiding parties — armed with huge mastiffs — from the encampment into the surrounding countryside to round up Indians for enslavement. While Columbus was not morally opposed to enslaving the Indians, he did not feel that it was in the best interests of the Spaniards to enslave the natives. He felt that it would be better to maintain friendly relations with the Indians until the colony was on a more solid footing. Given the attitude of the men at large, however, he had little choice but to give his approval to the slaving sorties.

Trade with the Indians proved disappointing, in part because the Indians did not have as much gold as the Spanish had hoped, and in part because the Spanish were unwilling to give the Indians anything more than trinkets in exchange for the gold. Within slightly more than two weeks of landing at Isabela, Columbus was forced to send twelve of his ships back to Spain in order to procure more provisions for the fledgling colony. From this point on, traffic between Spain and the Indies — ferrying food, supplies, men, letters, and whatnot — grew increasingly commonplace.

This first convoy journeying back to Spain contained a report that Columbus had prepared for

Ferdinand and Isabella; it was optimistic but frank. There was plenty of gold in the new land, Columbus wrote, but it was difficult to mine. He added that many of his men were sick because of the "change of water and air," but that they would regain their health once shipments of "the food to which they were accustomed in Spain" arrived. In addition, since most of the colony's livestock had died, cows, horses, and mules were needed. Clothing was also a problem. Columbus requested that the monarchs send shoes, cloth, and leather. Finally, Columbus wrote that the subjugation of the island would require more crossbows and muskets. If Isabella and Ferdinand wished, the island could serve as the center of a booming slave trade. Columbus would send their majesties as many slaves as they desired. Intrigued by the 60 parrots, 26 Indians, and 14,000 gold sovereigns Columbus sent along to pique their interest, the Catholic monarchs hastened to comply with his requests, although they told him to hold off on the slave trade for the present.

While Columbus awaited the return of the ships from Spain, he decided to explore. He was still convinced that he was not far from China. In late April he left his brother Diego in command at Isabela and took three caravels to the southern coast of Cuba, which he thought might contain the great cities he had been expecting. He spent some six weeks exploring the area, but found only deep forests, a series of lovely bays and harbors, and Indians. With provisions running low and his ships' sails in tatters, Columbus finally allowed his crew to persuade him to return. Before returning to the Spanish settlement at Isabela he made each one of them sign an affadavit testifying to their belief that Cuba was part of the continent of Asia.

Upon his return, Columbus was overjoyed and surprised at the sight of his brother Bartholomew, whom he had not seen in six years. Bartholomew had been in France, where he had first gone to try to secure aid for Columbus from the French king. Upon learning of the successes of his older brother's first voyage, Bartholomew had hurried to Spain but arrived after the departure of the second voyage. Fortunately, Ferdinand and Isabella's generosity extended to Columbus's brother as well, and he was outfitted with three caravels with which to carry provisions to Hispaniola.

Columbus's joy did not last long, for the situation at Isabela had deteriorated since his departure. Diego Columbus was even less well suited to governing a colony than Christopher, and he possessed none of his brother's charisma. Huge squadrons of well-armed Spaniards, two or three hundred strong, had taken to roaming the island's interior, pillaging and plundering Indian villages as they went. The Columbus brothers wished to control the interior to be sure that they and the Crown would receive their rightful share of any gold that was found. Diego Columbus sent word to Pedro Margarit, the leader of one of the renegade Spanish forces, telling him to cease mistreating the Indians. Margarit would not hear of it. Instead, he and his men marched on Isabela, commandeered Bartholomew's vessels, and sailed back to Spain. There they told Ferdinand and Isabela that for the good of the colony Columbus ought to be recalled.

Ferdinand and Isabella sent word to Columbus summoning him back to Spain. Columbus, however, felt that his mission in the Indies was not finished. Believing that Ferdinand and Isabella could be placated with slaves, he ordered the colonists to capture as many Indians as they could. In all, two thousand Indians were seized, despite the fact that only five hundred captives could fit aboard the vessels that were returning to Spain. The remaining Indian captives were divided among the colonists. Columbus then led an expedition of conquest across the island. Although the Indians outnumbered the Spaniards, in most instances they fled before the white men's horses, fierce dogs, and muskets — all of which were new and strange things to them. To enforce the conquest, Columbus instituted a system of forced tribute: each Indian was to provide a certain amount of gold each year. Penalties for failure to comply with this rule included flogging, enslavement, or death.

Still, the colonists remained unhappy. They continued to be unwilling to plant their own food, preferring to rely on the provisions that arrived irregularly from Spain. Hunger and disease were commonplace; only 630 of the original 1,200 colonists remained alive.

In addition to the provisions that they carried, the convoys from from Spain also brought news to

Columbus about his standing in the court. It was clear that Ferdinand and Isabella were displeased with the reports they were hearing about conditions in the Spanish settlement. Columbus realized he had best return to Spain, and left Bartholomew in charge of the colony. His parting advice to his brother was that he should abandon Isabela in favor of a more hospitable location.

Columbus's journey back to Spain was a grim one. There were few provisions, and Columbus placed the crew on a daily ration of six ounces of bread and a single cup of water. In June 1496, two years and nine months after he had left Spain on his second transoceanic voyage, Columbus landed at Cadiz. The crew staggered from the ships, weak and wasted with hunger. Columbus himself, suffering from arthritis and a high fever, had to be helped from the ship. Another triumphal cavalcade to the royal court was organized, but it seemed halfhearted in comparison with the first. Nevertheless, Ferdinand and Isabella seemed congenial, and after hearing Columbus's explanations for the problems on Hispaniola, they authorized him to outfit another voyage.

Columbus was now forty-five. His many trials had aged him beyond his years. Still, despite being weary and ill, he did not believe that his work was done, and he had no intention of retiring in Spain, as some of his friends suggested he do. He did take the time while away from the New World to analyze why things had not worked out exactly as planned at Isabela, and concluded that his own pride in the achievements of his first voyage had caused him to lose favor with the Lord. As a sign of repentance and humility, he donned the brown robe of a Franciscan monk, which became his customary garb.

It took more than a year to ready seven ships and recruit 300 colonists for the third voyage. Word of the problems on Hispaniola had spread. Few people now desired to settle there. In order to obtain colonists, the Catholic monarchs were forced to declare a general pardon for any criminals willing to colonize the Indies.

Columbus's third voyage across the Ocean Sea embarked in June 1498. He did not plan to sail directly to Hispaniola. Rather, he was now convinced, after rereading the writings of Aristotle and other ancient wise men, that the most valuable treasures were to be found south of the Equator. He steered his fleet farther south. After an uneventful ocean passage of six weeks' duration, Columbus reached land in late July. Having dedicated this voyage to the Holy Trinity, Columbus named the large island he had happened upon, with its three tall mountains, Trinidad. Further exploration brought him to the coast of what is now Venezuela, in South America. At first Columbus did not realize that he had discovered a new continent. It was only after several days' sailing along the Venezuelan coast that he realized this land was not the Indies. The stirring sight of the waters of the Orinoco River pouring into the sea convinced him that he had uncovered something magnificent and new. This land was not merely a province of China or Japan;

as he wrote in his journal: "I believe that this is a very great continent, until today unknown. And reason aids me greatly because of that so great river and fresh-water sea, and next, the sayings of Esdras . . . that the six parts of the world are of dry land, and one of water . . . and further am I supported by the sayings of many Carib Indians whom I took at other times, who said that to the south of them was mainland . . . and they said that in it there was much gold . . . And if this be a continent, it is a marvelous thing, and will be so among all the wise, since so great a river flows that it makes a fresh-water sea of 48 leagues."

Further consideration convinced Columbus that his discovery was even greater than he had supposed. Now he believed that he had sailed into the very Garden of Eden itself, and he cited the Bible's Book of Genesis to back up his claims. Genesis stated the the Garden was in the east part of Eden; Columbus believed he was at the easternmost point of the Far East. The Biblical garden was said to be watered by a four-mouthed river, and the Orinoco had four mouths. Genesis said of Eden that the trees there were "pleasant to the sight and good for food" and that "the gold of that land is good," assertions that corresponded with what Columbus knew of the lands he viewed.

Columbus then sailed northward to bring the good news of his discovery to Hispaniola, but the situation in the settlement there more closely resembled hell than paradise. Bartholomew had succeeded in moving the colony from Isabela to a new city he called Santo Domingo, but the same problems still existed. The men refused to build houses and were living in mud huts. No one would plant food, and exploitation of the Indians had worsened. Large groups of men had defied Bartholomew's orders and departed regularly for the interior to mine gold illegally. Even worse, Francisco Roldán, whom Columbus had appointed as the island's chief justice, had rebelled against the rule of these "cursed Genoans" and with a large band of followers seized a Spanish fort in the interior; he was planning to conquer Santo Domingo. Bartholomew and Diego had tried to restore order by imprisoning and hanging a few of the most notorious troublemakers, but that had just increased the unrest.

Columbus's arrival only made matters worse. The colonists blamed him for all their problems. Exhausted, stiff with gout and arthritis, and intoxicated with his mystical visions of the paradise on earth he had discovered, Columbus was in no shape to put things right. Meanwhile, back in Spain, Ferdinand and Isabella were deluged with complaints having to do with Hispaniola. Returning colonists insisted that Columbus was mad, that he had run amok and was hanging Spaniards left and right, that he heard voices and saw hallucinations. Each time they stepped out in public, Columbus's two sons were hounded by disillusioned colonists who screamed at them: "There go the sons of the Admiral of the Mosquitos, of him who discovered lands of vanity and delusion, the ruin and the grave of Castilian gentlemen." Having heard enough, the Catholic monarchs dispatched Francisco de Bobadilla to replace Columbus as viceroy and governor.

When De Bobadilla arrived in Santo Domingo, the first sight that greeted him was that of seven Spanish corpses swinging from the gallows. Diego Columbus, who had been left in charge of the settlement while Columbus and Bartholomew were off exploring the interior, cheerfully told de Bobadilla that five more Spaniards were to be hanged the following morning. An appalled Bobadilla arrested Diego and impounded all of Columbus's property. He then declared that all the colonists were free to gather gold wherever they pleased. When Columbus appeared a few days later, he, too, was seized, chained, and thrown into the brig of Bobadilla's ship. A similar fate befell Bartholomew. The three Columbus brothers were then shipped back to Spain for trial.

Thus ended Columbus's dreams for Hispaniola. As he wrote in a letter to a friend at court, despite the fact that he had discovered "a new heaven and a new earth," he was being returned to trial in chains and humiliated. He had suffered setbacks before. Indeed, he complained in his letter, the world's "custom of mistreating me is of very old standing." Now, however, his humiliation was so complete "that there is none so vile who dare not to insult me." Still, the feeble and enchained captain clung to hope. "Our Lord God lives, with His power and wisdom, as in the past, and above all things, He

punishes ingratitude and wrongs," Columbus
wrote. In this the intrepid mariner rested his faith.

8

The Last Voyage

A DIFFERENT MAN no doubt would have been broken by the ordeal, but not Columbus. He recovered much of his strength, and even seemed to derive power from his troubles. Columbus was simply not a man to give in to adversity. When the captain of the ship bearing Columbus back to Spain offered to remove his chains, the proud Genoan refused, saying that since his monarchs had ordered that they be fastened upon him, only his monarchs could undo them. When his chains were finally removed, Columbus asked that he be allowed to keep them so that they could be buried with him when he died.

Columbus and his brothers appeared before Ferdinand and Isabella just prior to Christmas, 1500. The tenor of their meeting was in sharp contrast to all the others that had taken place. Wan and thin, almost fifty years old, and somewhat stooped and slow moving, Columbus no longer exuded the same air of vitality and confidence that he had when he had first appeared before the sovereigns as a young man. His eyes, however, still burned with the same inner conviction.

The monarchs, too, were older. Isabella in particular was moved as Columbus, the strange Genoan who years ago had convinced her of his singularity, recited the injustices he felt had been done to him.

"For years I endured the jeers of all men, fools and knaves who laughed at my Enterprise of the Indies," he told the court. He spoke in a low monotone that was close to a whisper. "Many of them resided at this court. But in your infinite wisdom your highnesses listened to my pleas, and with the help of the Lord, I have seen and done remarkable things. God has seen fit to use me to fulfill the Biblical prophecy of the discovery of a new heaven and a new earth, and all that I have done has been done for Him and for Spain. I have done my adopted country great service; today she reigns over a vast and rich empire, and she is the envy of her neighbors. Yet I am brought back to her fair shores in chains, which wound my soul as surely as they damage my body, and am again the scorn of all men, even the lowliest beggar. All this occurs because those who I have given most cause to trust and honor me instead give greater credit to the vile lies and slanders of my enemies, who seek to profit themselves with my destruction."

Columbus bowed his head before Ferdinand and Isabella. He wore a frayed brown Franciscan robe;

Columbus in chains. Columbus fell into disgrace with both his men and his royal patrons because of troubles arising at Santo Domingo, the Spanish settlement on Hispaniola. Among other things, Columbus was blamed for there not being enough gold to make everyone "rich" within a year.

on his wrists, the marks of the chains that had ground into his flesh were clearly visible. Columbus had been beaten, but he was not yet broken. Remarkably, he had demands to make. He asked that the monarchs restore his titles of governor and viceroy and that he be allowed to mount another expedition to Hispaniola.

The king and queen delayed their decision for months. Isabella felt guilty about the way he had been treated; Ferdinand, on the other side, regarded Columbus as a nuisance. Finally, the monarchs informed Columbus that he would be given four ships with which to mount an expedition. Their support, though, was conditional. The titles of viceroy and governor would be restored to Columbus, but he would not be permitted to exercise them on the settlement of Hispaniola. In fact, he was expressly forbidden to land on Hispaniola, although he would be allowed to send an agent to try to retrieve the property, mainly gold, that de Bobadilla had seized from him. The monarchs told Columbus that de Bobadilla would be recalled from Hispaniola, but that Don Nicolas de Ovando, not Columbus, would replace him. In contrast to Columbus's's tiny fleet, de Ovando's mission would consist of thirty ships and 2,500 men.

In April 1502, Columbus set sail from Spain. He had persuaded Bartholomew to join him once again. Columbus's thirteen-year-old son Ferdinand was also among the crew, whose members were in awe of their fabled and somewhat infamous captain. To them it seemed that Columbus was able to converse with God. He navigated as if he were receiving messages from the heavens. Despite Columbus's feebleness — his arthritis had worsened, and he was prone to fever and delirium — his uncanny seamanship won his crew's respect, and they began calling him "the Divine."

Columbus intended to return to the South American lands that he referred to as "the other world." However, as he passed near Santo Domingo, he became aware from changes in the atmosphere that a great hurricane was blowing up. Knowing that Nicholas de Ovando was on the verge of sending a great fleet back to Spain, Columbus had his ships seek shelter in the mouth of a river and sent a message to de Ovando, the new governor, warning him of the impending tempest. De Ovando was distressed to hear that Columbus was near Hispaniola, but the Genoan's meteorological predictions amused him greatly. He read the admiral's warnings aloud to his cronies, who all roared with laughter and agreed that Columbus's mystical pretensions had gotten the better of him. The fleet left as planned. The storm arrived as Columbus had predicted. As the lightning flashed and the wind howled, Columbus pondered the irony of his situation. He wrote later to Ferdinand and Isabella: "What man ever born, not excepting Job, would not have died of despair when in such weather, seeking safety for son, brother, shipmates and myself, we were forbidden the land and the harbor that I, by God's will and sweating blood, won for Spain!" The hurricane struck Ovando's fleet with a righteous fury, sending nineteen of its twenty-four ships to the bottom and four more ships scurrying back to Santo Domingo. Ironically, only one vessel made it to Spain — the one carrying Columbus's gold, which his agent had succeeded in retrieving. Meanwhile, on Hispaniola, Ovando and his supporters now believed that Columbus possessed supernatural powers that he was using against them.

Columbus and his fleet waited until the hurricane lifted, then sailed westward along the southern coasts of Jamaica and Cuba and across the Caribbean Sea to the coast of what is now Honduras. Believing that he was now in the vicinity of the Malay peninsula in southeast Asia, Columbus searched for a strait that would carry him into the Indian Ocean and allow him to sail west all the way back to Spain.

But before Columbus could get very far, his small fleet encountered another storm. More ferocious than any he had ever withstood, it tormented the Spanish vessels for twenty-eight consecutive days and nights. As Columbus described it: "It was one continual rain, thunder and lightning. The ships lay exposed to the weather, with sails torn, and anchors, rigging, cables, boats, and many of the stores lost; the people exhausted and so down in the mouth that they were all the time making vows to be good, to go on pilgrimages and all that; yea, even hearing one another's confessions! Other tempests I have seen, but none that lasted so long or so grim as this. Many old hands whom we looked on as stout fellows lost their courage. What griped me most were the sufferings of my son; to think that so young a lad, only thirteen, should go through so much. But Our Lord lent him such courage that he even heartened the rest, and he worked as though he had been to sea all of a long life."

The ordeal of the storm almost destroyed Columbus. The wounds on his wrists and ankles from the chains reopened, and he bled substantially. Many times the crew believed he would die, but Columbus always rallied. In the next several months the fleet went on to explore the coasts of present-day Costa Rica, Panama, and Nicaragua. Columbus was too weak to go ashore and was reduced to giving orders from a small, doghouse-like shelter the crew built for him on deck.

As his body grew weaker, the spiritual side of Columbus's character grew stronger. On one occasion, when a funnel cloud threatened the ships, Columbus summoned all his will and rose to his feet. Seizing a Bible, he read aloud a passage from the Gospel story of Jesus's walking on the water. When he finished, he held the Bible aloft in his left hand and traced a giant cross in the sky with a sword. The funnel cloud passed harmlessly by; the sailors looked at their captain with amazement and a little fear. Another time, while his men engaged Indians in a fierce battle on shore, Columbus, who had remained aboard ship in a fever-induced state of delirium, climbed to the top of the tallest mast and began shouting to his men to return. Suddenly, he slipped into a trance and imagined that he heard the voice of God speaking to him, reminding him of all He had done for Columbus — as much for Columbus as He had done for the prophet Moses or King David. "Fear not; have trust; all these tribulations are written upon marble and are not without cause," Columbus imagined the Lord to say.

More tribulations lay ahead for Columbus. Despite his sorry physical state, he wished to continue exploring his new lands, which he believed to be richer in gold than Hispaniola. Howeer, the condition of his fleet forced him to turn back. All the ships were hopelessly riddled with shipworms, reducing their hulls to porous wrecks. One had already been abandoned after the battle with the Indians. Another had nearly sunk on the way back to Hispaniola, where Columbus hoped to make repairs. It, too, had to be left behind. With the remaining two vessels taking on water at an alarming rate and on the verge of sinking, Columbus headed for Jamaica instead. The ships barely made it. On June 25, 1503, Columbus ordered them run aground on a beach on the island's south shore.

Columbus and the 115 members of his crew remained on Jamaica for more than a year waiting to be rescued. The hulls of the ships served as forts and living quarters. The Spaniards behaved badly toward the natives, as they had on the other islands. As on Hispaniola, they were unwilling to get their own food, either by hunting, fishing, or planting. Fortunately, the Indians were friendly and were willing to supply the Spaniards with food.

When after some seven months they grew tired of feeding the Spanish, Columbus tricked them into continuing. Knowing that a full lunar eclipse was due to occur on the last night of February, Columbus told the Indians that God wanted them to feed the Spaniards and would soon show his anger at their reluctance to do so. When the moon disappeared from view that night, the terrified Indians begged Columbus to intercede with his god to restore the moon to its rightful place. He would do so, Columbus told them, only if the Indians promised to give the Spaniards all the food they needed. The Indians vowed to do so, the eclipse ran its course, and the Spaniards were relatively well fed for the remainder of their stay.

The Indians also provided the Spaniards with a canoe, which two sailors — Diego Méndez and Bartholomew Fieschi, a Genoan — used to make the 108-mile trip to Hispaniola and ask Nicholas de Ovando to send help. De Ovando, however, still feared Columbus and was content to let him stay on Jamaica forever. Finally, the sailors succeeded in chartering a ship from a captain who had previously sailed with Columbus to rescue Columbus and his men. Rescuers eventually reached Jamaica on June 29, 1504, over a year after the original shipwreck, and bore the survivors back to Santo Domingo. Among the survivors was the nearly fifty-three-year-old Columbus.

Despite his ordeal, Columbus lost no time in getting back to sea. In September, he and Bartholomew chartered a ship and sailed for Spain. Few other members of the crew who had originally set sail with him were as hearty. Only twenty-two joined him on the trip, the rest preferring to remain in Santo Domingo rather than risk another sea voyage.

Upon his return to Spain, a bitter Columbus learned that he had worn out his welcome. Isabella was dying, and Ferdinand refused to allow him to come to court. The king did not wish to hear about Columbus's last voyage, nor did he want to learn about Columbus's plans for future journeys. Even Columbus's men were treated poorly. Those who had returned to Spain with him were owed two years' wages, but the Crown simply refused to pay.

Columbus's health deteriorated steadily. His arthritis worsened, and most of the time he was confined to bed in rented homes. Still, he did not rest. He used what energy he had to petition Ferdinand to restore his titles and rights or to confer them upon his oldest son, Diego. Ferdinand instead offered a castle, lands, and a huge pension if Columbus agreed to relinquish all the rights promised him under the Capitulations. Proud to the last, Columbus refused, and he was given nothing.

Despite his protestations of poverty, Columbus had actually accumulated a small fortune in gold on his voyages. As death approached, he dreamed of using it to fund a naval expedition to free the holy lands of the Levant from their Muslim conquerors. Nothing would come of this plan, another among many he would never see fulfilled.

Columbus, the intrepid mariner, died at Valladolid, Spain, on May 20, 1506. The nation he had done so much to make a powerful empire scarcely noticed'his passing. The chronicle of the royal court made no mention of his death. A village priest, not a powerful bishop, recited the funeral mass. No emissaries from Ferdinand's court attended the burial. Columbus, the Admiral of the Ocean Sea, was lowered into his grave unaware of the magnitude of his discoveries. As befit the remains of a restless traveler, his body did not rest long in one place. It was moved several times before reaching its final resting place in the cathedral at Santo Domingo, in the New World.

Other books you might enjoy reading

1. Boorstin, Daniel J. *The Discoverers*. Vintage Books, 1985.

2. Humble, Richard. *The Explorers*. Time/Life Books, 1978.

3. Jane, Cecil, editor. *The Four Voyages of Columbus*. Dover Publications, 1988.

4. Maddocks, Melvin. *The Atlantic Crossing*. Time/Life Books, 1981.

5. Morison, Samuel Elliot. *Admiral of the Ocean Sea: A Life of Christopher Columbus*. Northeastern University Press, 1942.

6. Morison, Samuel Elliot. *The Great Explorers: The European Discovery of America*. Oxford University Press, 1986.

7. Morison, Samuel Elliot, translator. *Letter of Columbus on His Discovery of the New World*. University of Southern California, Fine Arts Press, 1989.

ABOUT THE AUTHOR

Sean Dolan has degrees in literature and history from the State University of New York. He is the author of a biography of Chiang Kai-shek, the Chinese leader, and has edited many books on historical subjects, including a series on world explorers past and present.

To Inspire and Capture the Imagination . . .

GREAT LIVES

BIOGRAPHY SERIES